SAINT JEROME

St. Jerome with St. Paula and St. Eustochium,
by Francisco de Zurbaran.

SAINT JEROME

The Sage of Bethlehem

CHARLES CHRISTOPHER MIEROW

THE BRUCE PUBLISHING COMPANY
MILWAUKEE

Library of Congress Catalog Card Number: 59–13488

FOR GLADYS

INTRODUCTION

ST. JEROME was, above all else, a scholar and a man of letters. His contemporary, St. Augustine, went so far as to say: "What Jerome is ignorant of no mortal has ever known." And Erasmus, centuries later, aptly calls him "the Christian Cicero," and characterizes him as "the divine Jerome . . . first of theologians." He is the unique example of a man who was canonized for his scholarship. The Latin Bible — the Vulgate version — is his greatest monument.

But Jerome was no dry-as-dust student and bookworm. He was always intensely alive, and was easily swayed by his feelings. His affections, his human traits and failings make Jerome more appealing to us than many other early leaders of the Christian Church.

As he could love deeply, so too he could hate with all the power of his being. He loved God. He loved Christian truth. He loved his Christian friends, and he was a man of many friends. But he hated error, especially error in matters of religious belief. He had a lifelong hostility to heretics. If a friend strayed from the path of orthodox belief, Jerome assailed the man because of the false doctrine. And he went to lengths of vilification not exceeded by the greatest of the Roman satirists. He had read them all.

So the story of his life is marked by paradox. Jerome

himself was not unaware of this. He comments on the incongruity of hiding his body in a desert or a monastery and permitting his voice to wander all over the world: for he was consulted as a sort of Christian oracle by visitors and letters from the whole of Europe. His enormous correspondence is the chief source for our knowledge of his personality and character.

Paradoxical, too, is his cosmopolitanism, when we recall that he lived for five years as a hermit in the desert of Chalcis and for thirty-five years in his cell at Bethlehem. His birthplace was not far from Aquileia, at the head of the Adriatic, a city that became the involuntary founder of Venice. He was educated in Rome and lived there again for three years in his prime. He had visited Athens, the ancient city of Salamis in Cyprus, and Alexandria in Egypt. Jerusalem was well known to him, and he lived for short periods in Antioch and in Constantinople. But he still called the desert his Paradise.

Jerome zealously preached celibacy and was, in fact, driven from Rome in 385 because of his views on this subject and his success in persuading many of the noble ladies of Rome to become nuns. "I know I am criticized," he says, "because I sometimes write to women!" A notable example of understatement. "But," he retorts, "if men would ask me questions about Scripture, I would not be writing to women." His lifetime association with a small group of devoted Christian women enabled him to accomplish the great work which occupied most of his life: the translation of the Bible from the original Hebrew and Greek into Latin. Paula, out of her great wealth, erected the buildings for a convent and a monastery at Bethlehem for the continuation of his Biblical endeavors. In addition to translating the Bible, he also composed extensive and important commentaries on its separate books. Jerome was still occupied with the commentary on Jeremiah at the time of his death in 420.

But to write the biography of such a man one must not merely be conversant with his voluminous writings. The 150 letters, to be sure, afford us the best insight into his mind and soul, but to understand him fully one should familiarize himself also with the places where he lived. It will be remembered that museums no longer present their exhibits without an appropriate background or setting.

The author has recently had the good fortune of visiting the Mediterranean and seeing for himself most of the places which Jerome knew in his lifetime. It was in Bethlehem that St. Jerome lived for the greater part of his life: thirty-five years. Not inappropriately, therefore, when I reached the Holy Land I visited first the Church of the Nativity and Jerome's cell in the cave adjoining the place accepted today as the spot where Jesus was born.

To Jerome and his devout friends, Paula and Eustochium, and perhaps to all Christians everywhere, it was the holiest spot on earth. "With what language, with what utterance," he asks, "can I describe to you the Saviour's cave? And that manger in which a little babe wailed must be honored rather by silence than by my feeble speech." But his exultation overcomes his natural reticence. "Behold," he says, "in this little hole in the ground the Creator of the heavens was born. Here he was wrapped in swaddling clothes; here he was seen by the shepherds; here he was pointed out by the star; here he was adored by the wise men." A similar sense of wonder is felt by every visitor to this holy place.

The Church of the Nativity, in form a Roman basilica that goes back to the reign of Constantine, has a surprisingly low door for an entrance: tradition declares that this is due to an unfortunate habit of the infidels during the Dark Ages of entering the church on horseback. The cave which is accepted as the birthplace of Jesus, and was so regarded before Rome became officially Christian, is directly below the high altar of the church. The cave is lighted by hanging lamps, and in the floor is set a silver star about which is an inscription in Latin reading: "Here Jesus Christ was born of the Virgin Mary."

Not far away is the rock chamber which became Jerome's cell, where he worked at his translation of the Bible. Just outside is the place where he was buried. Across from his tomb is that of his devoted pupils and friends, Paula and Eustochium.

Here, at the outset, we are introduced to perhaps the greatest desire in the heart of this saint of God: to become more Christlike by constant reflection upon Him "who, though he was by nature God, did not consider being equal to God a thing to be clung to, but emptied himself . . . being made like unto men." While humility was not always characteristic of Jerome's conduct, nevertheless it must have been a motive for his retirement from the world.

With a sense of expectation I descended a flight of stone steps into the antechamber largely occupied by two elaborate places of burial. They are wooden shrines, roofed over, and each adorned by a mural painting. Each has a recessed altar, a crucifix, and half a dozen candlesticks. The metal-covered tops of these tombs are decorated with geometrical designs made with brass headed nails, and from each depend hangings whose points are edged with gold tassels, surmounting a white lace valence. From the natural rock of the ceiling between the two shrines hangs a brass lamp.

The tomb on the left as one enters is the burial place of Paula and Eustochium, the mother and daughter who served in turn as heads of the convent. Both died before Jerome himself: Paula in 404 and Eustochium in 418. The picture above the tomb of the two Roman ladies is singularly fresh and lifelike, and represents them as lying side by side, with their hands folded across their bosoms. In the sky above them are cherubs that hold out the reward of faithfulness: the crown of life.

Directly opposite their elaborate shrine is the almost identical tomb where St. Jerome was buried. However, his bones were later removed to the great basilica St. Mary Major's, in Rome, where they were interred in the Sistine Chapel.

His original tomb, here in Bethlehem, is marked by the letters S.H.: *Sanctus Hieronymus,* surrounded by a wreath. The painting above the tomb, not as well preserved as that of his beloved pupils, represents him as an old man with a long beard, his hands folded on his bosom, his eyes closed in the slumber of death. An angel is portrayed in the clouds above him, perhaps Gabriel, with a trumpet to his lips.

As we enter the chamber which was his study for so many years, we are impressed by its stark emptiness. To be sure, there is here an elaborate marble altar with another portrait above it. In one wall there is a stained glass window showing the man of God in an attitude of prayer. Another more formal oblong window, bordered with the Greek meander pattern in ironwork, bears the inscription SACELLUM S. HIERONIMI surrounding the Cross of Jerusalem, which is also known as The Crusaders' Cross. Above the entrance doorway is a Latin inscription on a marble tablet, identifying the room on the authority of ancient tradition as the actual place where Jerome translated the Bible from its original tongues into Latin.

Here we have nothing of the charm of Albrecht Dürer's familiar engraving of St. Jerome in his study, nor of the spaciousness found in the painting of Antonello da Messina. But if we close our eyes, we may be able to conjure up a mental picture of the room as it looked when it contained the author's writing table, his chair, and his bookcases, and we may picture him to ourselves, seated at his customary task and wielding the pen that gave the world its Latin Bible.

Few men that have ever lived have written more or greater works than he. But in this account of his life we are trying to become acquainted with Jerome the man, not merely with Jerome the author.

Nor have I based my biography chiefly upon predecessors in the field. I have tried to let Jerome speak for himself. For he once said: "It is not by the brilliance of great men, but by my own strength, that I must be judged."

CONTENTS

Europe in the Fourth

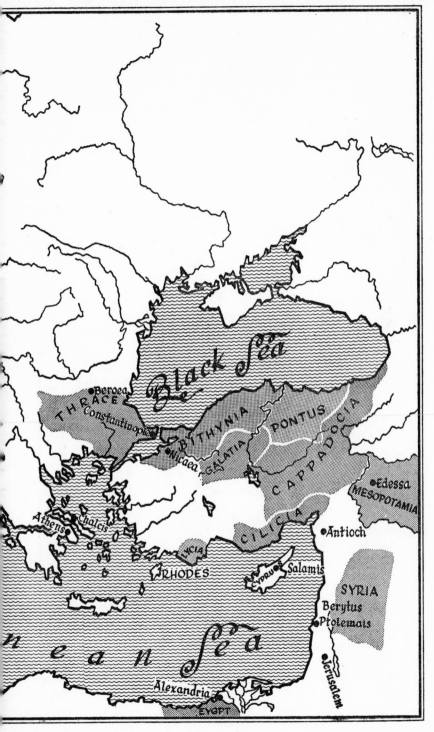

and Fifth Centuries

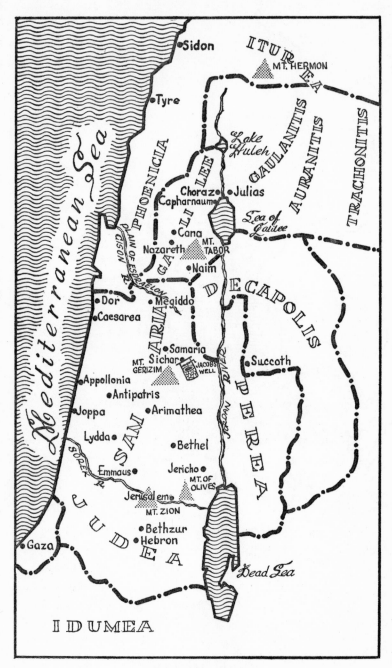

The Holy Land

SAINT JEROME

CHAPTER I - EARLY YEARS

THE date of Jerome's death is a matter of precise record, September 30, 420, at Bethlehem. He is said to have lived to his ninety-first year.

Yet he refers to himself as "only a boy," *adhuc puer*, in the year 363. If that means a boy of eighteen, he must have been born about 345 rather than in 330. Of course the difficulty lies in the changing attitude toward age which characterizes our common experience of life. In the year 374 Jerome wrote from the desert of Chalcis a letter in which he says: "Here an old man must either learn a barbarous tongue or maintain silence." "An old man" at twenty-nine, if he was born in 345! But twenty years later (in 394), in looking back to this same age and referring to another letter written in that very year, Jerome remarks: "When I was a young man — no, a mere boy!" Referring again to his solitary life in the desert in a letter he wrote (in 411): *Dum essem iuvenis*, "when I was a young man." Let us assume, then, that Jerome was born in or about the year 345.

It is no longer possible to visit the birthplace of St. Jerome. The house has long since vanished, and there is no stone set to mark the spot. Indeed, although we know the name of his native town, Stridon, we cannot even say exactly where it stood. The sole source of information we have about it is contained in his own statement concerning himself, in his list of Christian writers: "Hieronymus (his actual name), whose father was Eusebius, from the town of Stridon, which was destroyed by the Goths; once the tongue of land between Dalmatia and Pannonia." That is, he was born in Italy, in the Roman province of Venetia, and apparently not far from Aquileia, its capital city.

The modern traveler will search in vain for traces of this city also. We have in the Gothic History of Jordanes, written in 551, an interesting account of its destruction by the Huns under Attila in 452. Because of the stubborn resistance of its Roman garrison, the barbarian assailants, to whom anything so dull and prosaic as a siege seemed tedious and uninteresting, were about to revolt against their leader. Then Attila chanced to observe that the storks, contrary to their custom, were bearing their young out of the city, where they had built nests in the gables of the houses. Shrewdly availing himself of this fact, Attila said to his men: "You see the birds foresee the future. They are leaving the city sure to perish and are forsaking strongholds doomed to fall." The Huns made a last desperate assault, took Aquileia, and so cruelly devastated it as scarcely to leave a trace to be seen.

Refugees from Aquileia fled to the lagoons at the mouths of the Piave and the Brenta, occupying the islands which later became the site of the city of Venice. So not only Stridon, his birthplace, but the nearby city of Aquileia as well has vanished without a trace.

While he was a hermit in the desert of Chalcis, near Antioch, perhaps in the year 374, Jerome wrote in one of his letters to a friend in Aquileia: "For here, where I am now, I am ignorant, not merely of what is going on in my native land, but even whether my native land itself still exists." So he lost track of his home even before it was actually destroyed. In another letter, written twenty-two years later (in 396) from Bethlehem, Jerome mentions the incursions of the Huns in 395 as having started twenty or more years earlier. This may serve to cast light on the reason why, in those first months of loneliness in the desert, he could not be sure that the city of his birth was still in existence.

In another early letter from the desert of Chalcis he calls Stridon "that slave of rusticity," perhaps an ancient equivalent of our modern slang phrase "that hick town." He felt that the city was behind the times and too addicted to pagan superstitions. It is perhaps interesting to note in this connection that the Latin word *pagani* like our own "heathen" and the German "die Heiden" means "people of the heath," that is, the country folk. For it is in cities that new religions usually start. The countryside is more conservative. It is the people who are behind the times, who still observe old customs and cherish old beliefs, who are called "pagan" or "heathen."

His father's name, Eusebius, and his own, Hieronymus, would seem to indicate Greek ancestry. And, as a matter of fact, he was taunted as "that Greek, that impostor," in later years, in the time of his unpopularity in Rome. However, a younger brother was called by the characteristically Roman name, Paulinian. He had a sister whose name has not come down to us, and a foster brother named Bonosus.

Of the latter we know that he and Jerome had the same nurse, and that both were sent to Rome to complete their studies. One further piece of information about Jerome and Bonosus is that they lived together for a time "on the semi-barbarous banks of the Rhine."

There, apparently at Trier, in Germany, both young men decided to become hermits. This was after the completion of their studies at Rome. The two joined a band of ascetics at Aquileia, and when the group scattered Bonosus started his life as a hermit not far from home, on a small island off the Dalmatian coast. This news came to Jerome when he was in the desert of Chalcis. He writes to his correspondents (three friends of his own age): "You tell me that Bonosus — like a true son of the Fish — seeks watery places." The reference, of course, is to the use of the fish as an early symbol of Christianity. The letters of the Greek word for fish — I, ch, th, u, s — are the initials of the Greek words that mean "Jesus Christ, God's Son, Saviour."

From all this we infer that Jerome's father was a man of considerable means, and that he, like the father of Horace, the Roman poet, desired the best possible education for his children. Jerome's education was started at home, and we know that the family fortune permitted the employment of a nurse and other household servants. In his response to a work written by his boyhood friend Rufinus, Jerome said: "I remember that as a boy I once ran through the servants' quarters, spent a day in idleness and play, and was finally captured and dragged from the refuge of my grandmother's bosom back to my angry tutor." The impression given by the implications of this sentence is that of a wealthy home and a doting grandparent. Elsewhere Jerome refers to the fact that children learn the use of bad language from servants.

So much for the tantalizingly meager allusions which he makes to his childhood at home.

The education desired by Eusebius for his two sons was to be had in the world's capital at Rome; the city on the seven hills was a thousand years old long before Jerome was born. Rome was the natural place for a young man of his time to study, surrounded on every side by the memorials of a past greatness that had made this city ruler of the world. Here, while the Republic still existed, the great orator Cicero had won his triumphs. Here in the days of Vergil and Horace the young Octavius, adopted by Julius Caesar as his son and heir, had become the first Emperor of a realm that was to endure for another five hundred years. To Rome accordingly Jerome was sent by his father, with Bonosus, probably in the year 354.

To be sure there had been many changes in the centuries that had elapsed since the days of Romulus and Remus. The kingdom that was founded with the building of the city itself in 753 B.C. had lasted for some two hundred fifty years, to be succeeded in 509 B.C. by the Roman Republic. Half a millennium later, in the battle of Actium, Octavius — by the terms of Julius Caesar's will, adopted as his son and styled Gaius Julius Caesar Octavianus — had prevailed over the fleet of Antony and Cleopatra and made himself sole ruler of Rome. His reign, starting in that year of 31 B.C., had continued for 45 years. While he was Emperor, Jesus was born in Bethlehem in the obscure province of Judea across the sea. During the reign of his successor, Tiberius, the Crucifixion occurred. Oddly enough as it seems to us, all the historian Tacitus has to say of this period in the history of the Holy Land is *sub Tiberio quies* — "under Tiberius there was peace."

Yet the new faith that was spread by St. Paul and other apostles and martyrs during the first century of the Christian era ultimately became the official religion of the Roman Empire. In 313 the great Constantine, the first Christian Emperor, had issued an edict of toleration, and in 325 he had called the first general council of the Church at Nicea in Bithynia.

When Jerome came to Rome a generation later, it was still a pagan city, however. He speaks of the cobwebs which he saw in the dingy temples of forgotten gods; yet the temples themselves were still there. Many who opposed the new religion believed that the military reverses increasingly suffered by the Roman Empire were to be attributed to defection from the old gods. Their names were legion. Aside from the Olympian deities there were the native nymphs of trees and fountains; the deities of mountain and stream; the gods of the fields and harvest. As foreign lands were conquered and their peoples enslaved the number of the temples at Rome gradually increased. Here the Great Mother of the Gods from Pergamum was worshiped. Isis had her Egyptian devotees at Rome. Soldiers paid their vows to Mithras or worshiped The Unconquerable Sun. Nevertheless Rome had been, since Constantine, nominally Christian.

Jerome refers to himself as "a Christian, the son of Christian parents," although he had not yet been baptized when he came to Rome. As sins committed after baptism were considered more serious than the lapses of unregenerate youth, parents were inclined to postpone baptism. Neither Jerome nor his contemporary Augustine had been baptized in infancy or in childhood. We know that Jerome continued as a catechumen (to use the technical term for one preparing to be an acknowledged Christian) until Easter Sunday of 366, when he was baptized by Pope Liberius.

These two young boys, Jerome and Bonosus, and their friends and fellow countrymen, Rufinus of Concordia and Heliodorus of Altinum, must have seen much to fascinate and to impress them as they walked the city streets amid countless reminders of an earlier time. Doubtless, too, they inspected the ancient black stone still to be seen near the arch of Septimius Severus in the Roman forum. Not far distant was the Temple of Castor and Pollux with its memories of the Battle of Lake Regillus, another reminder of the days of the Roman Kingdom. When they walked along the banks of the Tiber they must have seen the mouth of the Cloaca Maxima, the great sewer that dates back to the time of the Tarquins, the Etruscan builders of The Eternal City.

As Christians they may have visited the ancient prison adjoining the forum, the Tullianum, or as it was called in the Middle Ages, the Mamertine Prison. Here Jugurtha and Vercingetorix and the Romans implicated in the conspiracy of Catiline, during Cicero's consulship in 63 B.C., had all met their death. Here, too, St. Peter was once imprisoned. They probably had entered the Basilica Julia, where St.

Paul had been tried and condemned. We know that on Sundays these young students walked out to the Catacombs outside the city to visit the tombs of the martyrs. What is more likely than that they also took a longer walk some day past St. Paul's Outside the Walls to see his place of execution, where the Tre Fontane are now pointed out to the tourist? Surely the Colosseum must have had a horrible fascination for them, as for all Christians.

And there were, of course, many more exciting forms of recreation, for Rome even in its tarnished magnificence of these later years offered much that was tempting to youth. There were races, processions, and gladiatorial games to be seen.

In later years, in a letter to Eustochium in which he refers to his experiences as a monk in the desert, he says: "O how often, in that vast solitude, I thought myself amid the delights of Rome." And more specifically: "I, who from fear of hell had condemned myself to such a prison, was often surrounded by dancing girls." In the Rome of his boyhood there had doubtless been voluptuous shows and many an invitation to sinful living. In fact, he says in another letter written from the desert to friends at home: "You yourselves know how slippery is the path of youth — whereon I fell and you make your way not without fear."

Yet it was for study that they had all come to Rome. In his *Chronicle*, in an entry for the year 354, Jerome speaks of Victorinus and Donatus as renowned in Rome, and refers specifically to the latter as "my teacher." Donatus had written a celebrated Latin Grammar, and Commentaries on the Comedies of Terence, and on Vergil. Perhaps we may assume that these works were used as textbooks in his classes.

During these early years as a student in Rome, Jerome became familiar with the works of the greatest Latin writers of the past. It was then that he read and committed to memory many favorite passages to be found in Plautus and Terence, in the *De rerum natura* of Lucretius, in Vergil, Horace, Persius, and Lucan. In prose, the books he studied included Cicero, of course, and Sallust. We know this from a passage in which he lists these authors for his boyhood friend and fellow student, Rufinus. But, of course, we would be able to learn the extent of his reading equally well by noting the frequent quotations from classical Latin literature contained in his writings.

During his later years, at Bethlehem, Sulpicius Severus (who visited him there) said of Jerome: "He is always reading, always buried in books: he doesn't rest day or night; he's always either reading something or writing something." This activity was the fruit of his student days.

Rhetoric as well as grammar and literature was an important part of his education. Jerome mentions the fact that he studied the three kinds of oratory: demonstrative, deliberative, and judicial. In fact, he sometimes had nightmares in which he found himself making a speech in the presence of his rhetoric teacher! "And when I wake up," he says, "I congratulate myself that I've been rescued from the dangers of public speaking." In connection with his study of speech he attended legal trials at Rome. There he discovered that deception rather than truth seemed to be the aim of the advocate.

His own writings clearly show that he profited greatly by his education in the field of language and literature. His knowledge of dialectics proved valuable when he composed his polemical treatises in later life. He appears not to have had the interest in philosophy and theology that was so distinguishing a trait of St. Augustine. Jerome was, rather, a scholar, a controversialist, and a man of letters.

Besides all this there was the normal social life of a student community, including student pranks. We have, for example, the anecdote of a lecture attended by Jerome and his friend Pammachius, in the course of which the speaker quoted a famous saying of Cato: *"Sat cito si sat bene."* — "It's soon enough done if it's well enough done." Jerome tells us that the whole audience burst into a spontaneous roar of laughter, amused perhaps by the awkward sound of the successive sibilants in the Latin phrase. Then with one accord they all shouted in unison: *"Sat cito, si sat bene!"* Such a thing might well happen in a modern classroom.

Perhaps Jerome's parents had planned to prepare him for government service after his years of education in Rome. At all events, we know that he went with Bonosus to Trier in Gaul in the year 367. This city had become the seat of government for the western Roman empire under Valentinian I.

However, Jerome was first and foremost a student. He had begun to collect a personal library during his student years, and we know that at Trier he copied with his own hand certain other books in which he was interested, including a volume by Hilary on the councils of the Church.

This journey into Gaul gave him an opportunity for travel and sight-seeing as well as for further study. Probably he took this occasion to visit its important cities, such as Mainz, Strassburg, Speier, Amiens, Tournai, Rheims, and Toulouse; in fact he must have seen at least some of them.

As might have been expected, Jerome studied the native language of the people of Gaul. Years later he mentions the fact (in his commentary on Paul's Epistle to the Galatians) that the speech of this people of Asia Minor is practically the same as that of the people of Gaul.

While he was in Brittany, moreover, Jerome appears actually to have encountered a tribe of cannibals! Thus, varied were his activities immediately after his school days. There is no record of his applying for an appointment in the Roman government, however. On the contrary, he soon began to feel a sense of vocation. It was not to any earthly ruler, but to Christ, that he decided to devote himself. He was perhaps influenced by a number of outward circumstances in making so momentous a choice. To begin with, it was in Trier that the great Athanasius had lived in exile from 335 to 337. From his reading, also, Jerome was familiar with the life of the first cenobite — "dweller in the wasteland" — whose biography had been written by Evagrius, afterward bishop of Antioch. Perhaps, then, it was the cumulative effect of these various influences in the course of this visit to Trier that induced both Jerome and Bonosus to withdraw from society and devote themselves to the celibate life.

We are not expressly informed what the reaction of his parents was to Jerome's decision. But we may perhaps conclude that it was not received with any great enthusiasm, particularly if he had disappointed their hopes and anticipations of a brilliant career.

Jerome himself makes a rather odd statement in alluding to his great decision. He says: "For the sake of the kingdom of heaven, I had cut myself off from my home, my parents, my sister, my kinsmen and — what was even more difficult — from an accustomed habit of good living." Apparently the contrast between his youthful home life and the loneliness and stark simplicity of the hermit's existence in the desert, far from ordinary human fellowship, was a great one.

Having decided what their future was to be, the two young men made their way homeward, going next to Aquileia, not far from Stridon, where they joined a company of ascetics. Jerome's friend Rufinus was also a member of this group. Many of them were clergymen. In his *Chronicle* for the year 373 Jerome says: "The clerics of Aquileia are considered to be a company of the blessed." Let us see who they were.

We may discover the names of some, at least, of the members of this group by noticing to whom Jerome writes his first letters from the desert. So, for example, the seventh letter (in Hilberg's edition) is sent "To Chromatius, Jovinus and Eusebius." It begins with the following words: "A sheet of paper ought not separate those whom mutual love has united."

Chromatius, whose home was the meeting place for "the company of the blessed," seems to have been the leading spirit. Eusebius was his brother, and the archdeacon Jovinus a mutual friend. It is interesting to note that all three eventually became bishops. Chromatius, as bishop of Aquileia, afterward ordained Jerome's friend Rufinus. We have also the names of others who are known to have been members of this pioneer group: the monk Chrysocomas (whose name perhaps bears witness to Germanic ancestry), Julian, a deacon, and the subdeacon Niceas, who in later years undertook a pilgrimage to Jerusalem.

As was only natural with a company of "solitaries," or hermits, they were soon separated from one another. Jerome wrote to Rufinus in those youthful years when they were still on terms of intimate friendship: "After that sudden storm tore me from your side, after that wicked rending asunder separated us (though I clung with the bond of affection) then 'Black was the stormy cloud that gathered above my head!'" Then there were "seas on every hand, and on every hand the sky." We shall hear again of Rufinus.

As has already been said, Jerome's foster brother, Bonosus, soon went off to his lonely island. The one member of the group who cast in his lot with Jerome and accompanied him to the desert of Chalcis was Heliodorus of Altinum.

Two others who exercised great influence over Jerome as a young man were Evagrius of Antioch and a youth called Innocent. The former first induced Jerome to write. Evagrius had come to the West with his friend Bishop Eusebius of Vercellae, who was returning from exile. He had attended a synod in Rome in 369 and was influential with Pope Damasus, who afterward became Jerome's friend and urged him to revise the Latin version of the Bible. In 373, when the group of ascetics scattered, Evagrius apparently persuaded several of them to accompany him to the Near East, going first to Antioch. So Evagrius, Jerome, Innocent, Heliodorus, Niceas, and Hylas were traveling companions. The last named was a slave of Melania, the wealthy Roman lady who became the friend and patron of Rufinus.

So Jerome began his life's career.

CHAPTER II · THE DREAM AND MALCHUS THE CAPTIVE MONK

WHEN he made his decision to become a monk — a hermit in the desert — Jerome was consciously and deliberately choosing hardship instead of a sheltered life, poverty instead of riches, loneliness instead of an assured place in the society of his peers. The hardship began with a long overland journey to the deserts of Asia Minor. Under the guidance of Evagrius, he and his comrades in the great venture made their way through Thrace and through Bithynia in Asia Minor; thence onward through Galatia, Pontus, Cappadocia and "the burning heat of Cilicia" — where Cicero once served as pro-consul or governor during the closing years of the Roman Republic. Here, in Cilicia, the little company stopped to visit Abbot Theodosius of Rhossus, to whom Jerome afterward wrote from his desert retreat. The goal of their journey was the great city of Antioch, where "the followers of the way" had first been called Christians, as is recorded in the book of *The Acts*. When they finally arrived, Jerome was ill and discouraged. "O how I wish I were now present in your convent," he writes to Theodosius. His distress and loneliness are evident in every word he writes, e.g., "I am like a sheep that is ill wandering away from the whole flock." Perhaps he regrets his irrevocable choice, for he says further: "I have not yet begun to put from me the allurement of my former riotous living." He finds himself in a dilemma: "I do not wish to go back and I cannot go forward."

The situation was even more serious than he knew. While Jerome lay sick in the home of his friend Evagrius, in Antioch, his close friend Innocent and the slave Hylas both died of the fever contracted on the journey. Heliodorus, another friend, had gone on alone to Jerusalem. Rufinus and his saintly patroness Melania were also making their way to Jerusalem, by way of Egypt. The subdeacon Niceas had given up and gone home. In writing to him, Jerome said: "You, who have so recently left me, are rending our friendship asunder rather than unstitching it — which Laelius wisely says should not be done." Evidently (as we note from the mention of Laelius) Cicero's familiar essay, "Laelius on Friendship," was, like many another favorite classic, a part of Jerome's mental equipment, impressed upon his memory by his education in the Eternal City.

Jerome begs his friends to write to him and cries in his despair that he wishes that the Lord would come and say to him as he lies in the tomb of his sins: "Hieronymus, come forth!" as once He had called Lazarus back from the dead.

During this period of loneliness and despondency Jerome, having recovered from his illness, heard Apollinaris of Laodicea speak in Antioch. He was greatly impressed by him and became his pupil, studying both Greek and the principles of exegesis (or the interpretation of the meaning of Scripture) under his guidance.

Jerome was a born student and could profit by the instruction of any scholar. Moreover, he was willing to learn important techniques even from those whose orthodoxy was questioned. He was doubtless also gaining a speaking knowledge of the Syrian tongue that was current there. Indeed, Jerome had few peers as a linguist.

His plans for the future were still somewhat vague and indefinite, but, of course, they included a trip to the Holy Land, now so near by. "I was going to Jerusalem to be a soldier of Christ." "But I could not do without the library which I had collected for myself at Rome, by great care and effort."

Books, however indispensable, are apt to become a burden to the traveler or to one who is changing his place of residence. Moreover, St. Francis of Assisi felt that it is impossible for one who owns books to persevere in the profession of poverty. "If you have books, you will need a bookcase," he said: "and if you have a bookcase you will need a house."

Jerome's qualms about owning and reading books went even deeper than this thought, however. The education he had received at Rome was, of course, a thorough grounding in what was called pagan literature. Was it right for a Christian to take delight in the works of Vergil and of Horace? This question troubled him greatly. "What has Horace to do with the Psalter," he cries, "Vergil with the Gospels, Cicero with Paul?" Moreover, to one as thoroughly trained as he was in the classics of ancient Greece and Rome, the style of the Bible appeared rude and lacking in polish. He tried to cultivate a taste for Scripture but (he tells us): "When I came to myself and had begun to read the prophet again, I rebelled at the uncouth style." He loved the ancient Roman writers and felt that he could not give them up. "After frequent night vigils," he tells us, "after shedding tears which the remembrance of past sins brought forth from my inmost heart, I would take up my Plautus."

One of the most famous and best known episodes in Jerome's life is the story of a dream which serves to make clear the conflict that raged within him: how to reconcile the new religion with the old culture. "In about mid-lent," he reports, "a fever attacked my enfeebled body and spread to my very vitals. . . . Preparations for my funeral were being made. My body was already cold. The vital warmth of life still throbbed feebly only in my poor breast." It was in this extremity that he had a dream — or a vision. "Suddenly I was caught up in the spirit before the seat of Judgment." There was a dazzling white light. He cast himself upon his face and dared not look up. A voice inquired what his status in life was. "I am a Christian," replied Jerome. "Thou liest," was the stern rejoinder: "Thou art a Ciceronian, not a Christian."

It was in the stress of that dark hour that Jerome cried out (but, be it observed, in his dream): "O Lord, if ever again I possess worldly books or read them, I have denied Thee."

Rufinus, who had been told of the dream, afterward accused him of breaking this promise, calling him forsworn. For, of course, Jerome did not forsake the reading of pagan literature. How could he? His mind was so stored with the beauties of the greatest writers of the Roman past that there are reminiscences of Cicero or of Vergil on almost every page he ever wrote. Eventually he learned that he could use his classical training in the service of Christ — and did so.

To be sure, Jerome does say that the pagan writings, and I suppose he is thinking especially of such writings as the comedies of Plautus and of Terence, are to be avoided "for the sake of weaker brethren." For how can a professing Christian exclaim, like the characters of Plautus, "Almighty Jupiter" or use such a petition as "So help me, Hercules!" It appears that even in profanity the Christian is expected to be different from the pagan! When he says "Damn" he must use that expletive in its proper Christian sense!

During the five years from 374 to 379 Jerome lived as a hermit in the desert of Chalcis, not far from the city of Antioch. Here he gave himself over to prayer and fasting, deeply penitent for the sins of his youth.

But Jerome was aware of the temptation which besets a man under these conditions of life. Looking back upon this experience in later years, he writes: "In solitude pride pounces swiftly upon a man. If he has seen no human being, he thinks himself of some account." He discovered also that fasting may be carried too far. Nor does loneliness or a new home necessarily bring escape from temptation or from sinful thoughts. As Horace so effectively puts it: "What exile from home has ever escaped from himself as well!" And Jerome himself tells us: "When I was a young man, and the desert surrounded me by its solitude as by a wall,

I could not withstand the promptings of sin and my ardent nature. Although I tried to subdue it by frequent fasting, yet my mind seethed with unruly imaginings."

He decided that to undertake a difficult task, like the mastery of the Hebrew language, might prove helpful. Thus Jerome became the first Latin father and, after Origen, the second father of the universal Church who knew and understood the language in which the Old Testament was written.

Thus he was being prepared, though unwittingly, for the great task he was destined to perform — the translation and elucidation of Scripture. For this a thorough grounding in Greek, in Hebrew, and in the fundamental principles of exegesis was indispensable.

MALCHUS, THE CAPTIVE MONK

In order to discover what conditions of life in the desert were like during the five years of Jerome's stay there, and in the generation just preceding his coming, we have only to read an early work of his entitled "The Life of Malchus, the Captive Monk." The general location is made clear by the story itself. "Maronias, a little village of no great distinction, is about thirty miles distant from Antioch, the Syrian city, to the eastward," says Jerome. And he continues: "While I was living in Syria as a young man, this village, after many previous lords and patrons, came into the possession of my friend, Father Evagrius. The reason why I now mention his name is to show how I came to know what I am about to write."

There is no reason to doubt that Jerome is telling the

truth. This is an autobiography recorded and published by an interested man of letters, not an imaginary tale.

"There was there" (that is, in Maronias), says Jerome, "a certain old man, Malchus by name (whom we might call in Latin *Rex*), a Syrian by race and speech as he was actually a native of that same place. There was also to be seen in his company an old woman, very feeble and already very close to death. Both were so earnestly religious, and so wore away the threshold of the church, that you might have taken them for Zacharias and Elizabeth out of the Gospel — except that John was not with them."

Becoming interested in them, Jerome first inquired of the neighbors, who declared that they were saints, and then approached Malchus himself. The remainder of the tale is given in his own words.

"My son," Malchus said to Jerome, "I was a small farmer at Maronias, and my parents' only child." As he was the only child, his parents were anxious to have him marry to continue their family. But he was determined to become a monk, and forsook his home and his parents in order to preserve his chastity.

"I came to the desert of Chalcis," says Malchus, "which is situated between Immae and Beroea, somewhat to the south." Beroea is known to us today as Aleppo, the region where Jerome became a hermit in the year 374.

After Malchus had lived for a number of years with a community of monks whom he found already established, having heard that his father was dead, he decided to return home to console his widowed mother. He planned to claim his inheritance and to divide the proceeds into three parts: one third for the poor, one third for the erection of a monastery, and the remainder for himself.

The abbot of the order to which he belonged remonstrated with him, declaring that this was clearly a temptation of the devil. But Malchus had made up his mind to depart. So he joined a caravan of seventy persons that he might travel homeward in safety. "As one travels from Beroea to Edessa, there is a desert near the public highway. Through it the Saracens wander hither and thither, never having fixed abodes.

"And lo!", continues the aged narrator of this tale of adventure, "suddenly the Ishmaelites dashed up, seated upon horses and camels, their hair long and bound with headbands, their bodies half naked, wearing flowing robes and broad boots. [The costume of the modern Arab has not changed greatly from that here described — even when they carry briefcases and ride in taxis! This, however, was a raiding party of the Bedouin of the desert.] Quivers hung from their shoulders; they brandished unstrung bows and carried long spears; for they had come not to fight but to secure booty. We are assailed, dispersed, dragged off in various directions."

Malchus continues: "Meanwhile I, the claimant of an inheritance after a long absence from home, repenting too late of my decision, with another — a young girl — became, by chance of the lot, slaves of one master. We are led away — nay, are carried aloft on camels — and through a vast desert, always fearing a fall, we cling to the creatures rather than ride them."

They crossed a great stream, perhaps the Euphrates, and

reached their destination in the interior, an extremely hot grazing country. Here he was given flocks to tend and lived a lonely life, as shepherds in the East do. "I seemed to myself to have some resemblance to the sainted Jacob; I remembered Moses; both of whom were once shepherds in the open country themselves. I lived on fresh cheese and milk. I prayed without ceasing and sang Psalms which I had learned in the monastery. My captivity was a delight to me; and I gave thanks to the judgment of God that I had found in the desert that life as a monk which I would have lost in my native land."

After a time his master sought to reward him for his faithfulness by giving him as a wife the female slave who had been captured with him. His protestations were of no avail. The owner of the slaves drew his sword "and," says Malchus, "had I not straightway anticipated him by clasping the woman in my arms, he would have shed my blood on the spot."

That night, in the solitude of the cave that provided them a home, Malchus decided to commit suicide rather than become a bridegroom. For "of what avail to have forsaken parents, country and patrimony for the Lord, if I do this thing, to refrain from doing which I forsook them?"

So he drew his sword, determined to die, and said to his intended bride: "Farewell, unhappy woman; have me as martyr rather than as husband." But the lady surprised him by declaring that she, too, would rather die than marry him! Accordingly they agreed to be partners in chastity while pretending to be man and wife. This satisfied their owners.

After a time, however, the two determined to make an attempt to escape. "I had in my flock two he-goats, of unusual size. These I killed and made bags of their skins. Their flesh I prepared as food for the journey. Early in the evening, when our masters thought that we were asleep in our retreat, we took to the road carrying the bags and part of the flesh. And when we had come to the river (it was ten miles distant) we inflated the bags of skin and, resting our weight upon them, entrusted ourselves to the water, little by little, striking out with our feet, so that as the current carried us downstream and set us on the other side far beyond the place where we had entered, those who followed us might lose the trail."

Thereafter they traveled by night, both to avoid the Saracens and because of the ardent heat of the desert sun. "Poor wretch that I am!" says Malchus. "I shudder at the very recollection. Although I have nothing to be anxious about, yet I tremble from head to foot."

Three days after their escape, the fugitives saw in the distance two men on camels. Finding a cave that ran down far below the earth, "at the very entrance we entrusted ourselves to a pit on the left." Soon their master and one of their fellow slaves, following their tracks in the sand, came to the entrance of the cave. "O how much worse is death when anticipated than when inflicted!"

The slave is sent to fetch them. He cries: "Come out, you gallows birds, come out to die."

Suddenly a lioness, in a deeper cavern, leaped upon the man and dragged him into the darkness by the throat. "Dear Jesus, what terror then was ours — and what joy!"

When his master entered, sword in hand, in search of his slave, he met a like fate.

In the morning the lioness carried her cub out of the place, leaving the den to Malchus and the woman. At nightfall they also went out, found the camels and provisions for a journey. Ten days later they reached a Roman camp in Mesopotamia where they received a price for the camels.

"And because that abbot of mine had already fallen asleep in the Lord, being brought to this place — that is, Maronias — I rejoin the monks. This woman I entrust to the nuns, loving her as a sister, yet not trusting myself to her as to a sister."

This story of Malchus the Captive Monk was written down by Jerome in A.D. 390. It has a moral and is connected with Jerome's lifelong ideal. The author says at the close: "This is the tale that the old man Malchus related to me in my youth. This I, as an old man, have narrated to you. I set forth to the chaste a record of chastity. I exhort maidens to preserve their virginity. Do you narrate it to your posterity, that they may know that purity is never taken captive amid swords and amid deserts and wild beasts, and that the man dedicated to Christ may die but cannot be vanquished."

CHAPTER III - LIFE IN THE DESERT, 374-379

So LONG as he lived, there were two main themes of Jerome's preaching and teaching: celibacy and the ascetic life. For five years of his life, from 374 to 379, he put his theories to the test by becoming a hermit in the desert of Chalcis, in Asia Minor. At the outset, he felt that he was in paradise.

However it was a lonely paradise; and Jerome, more than most men, needed human companionship. Moreover his closest friends, especially in his later years, were women.

His loneliness is clearly revealed to us in the first letters he sent from the desert to his loved ones at home. He declares that his rejoicing over the receipt of a joint letter from three friends was greater than that of the Romans when Marcellus, the Sword of Rome, first defeated Hannibal at Nola, in the days of the second Punic war. To him this comparison with an event that took place 600 years before did not seem in the least unusual, for Jerome had a remarkably detailed knowledge of the facts of ancient history, and his acquaintance with great men of old was comparable with that of other men with their contemporaries.

"Now I carry on a conversation with your letter," he writes in reply. "I embrace it; it speaks to me. It's the only thing here that understands Latin. For here an old man must either learn a barbarous manner of speaking or else remain silent."

"An old man" at the age of 29 — if he was born in 345! To be sure, we are all aware of the changing attitude toward age which characterizes our common experience of life.

To return to the letter that reached him during his first days in the desert: "As often as your familiar handwriting brings your dear faces to mind, so often am I not here — or you are here. Believe love when it speaks the truth: as I write this letter also, I see you." At the close his deep affection for his friends is again seen, when he says: "The brief compass of a letter compels me to be silent. Longing for you forces me to speak. My words pour forth with precipitate haste. My speech is confused and disjointed. Love knows nothing about order."

In these early periods of loneliness he found solace in frequent visits from Evagrius, the friend at whose instigation he had left his home and come to the East. Nevertheless he says: "Though the aforesaid brother often pays me a visit and cherishes me in Christ like his own flesh and blood, yet he is separated from me so far that he always plunges me into as great regret by his departure as he had brought me joy by his coming."

This was no merely temporary unhappiness; apparently his homesickness and longing for absent friends increased rather than diminished with the passage of time. In a famous letter, which the wealthy Roman matron Fabiola afterward committed to memory, Jerome deplores the apos-

tasy of his friend Heliodorus, who, having put his hand to
the plow, looked back, saying: "With how great enthusiasm
and love I urged that we should remain together in the
desert, your heart, conscious of our affection for each other,
fully realizes. With what lamentations, with what groaning,
I hailed your departure, even this letter to you is a witness:
you see it is blotted with tears."

This fervent appeal to his boyhood friend, though un-
successful in its purpose, was greatly admired by Jerome's
friends as a classic on the ascetic life. As a highly rhetorical
composition, it bears witness to the effectiveness of his
training at Rome. Jerome asks Heliodorus: "Why are you,
a Christian, so lacking in spirit?" And he continues: "Remember him who left his father as well as his nets; remember the publican who arose from receipt of custom, becoming an apostle at once." He points out that he can speak
from experience: "As one lately cast ashore after shipwreck,
I give advice, with timid voice, to those about to set sail.
In that boiling flood the Charybdis of luxury swallows up
our salvation. There lust, with a smile like that of Scylla on
her girlish lips, by flattery seeks to lure us to make shipwreck of our chastity. On this side is a savage coast, on
this a devil with his pirate crew bears chains for those to
be taken captive."

The reason why Heliodorus forsook his original intention
of becoming a monk was that he might enter the regular
clergy; which he did later. Jerome remarks: "If the pious
flatteries of the brethren invite you to take holy orders, I
shall rejoice at your elevation — and shall fear a fall!" And

again he says: "Ecclesiastical rank does not make a Christian. . . . Sit down in a lower place, brother, that when a lesser person comes you may be bidden to go up higher."

Then Jerome waxes eloquent in his description of the attractions of the wilderness. "O desert of Christ, burgeoning with flowers!" This, of course, is a true picture of springtime in the desert, with dark red anemones forming a carpet everywhere among the very boulders. "O Solitude," he adds, "in which those stones are produced of which in the Apocalypse the city of the great king is constructed! O wilderness that rejoices in intimacy with God. What are you doing in the world, brother — you who are greater than the world? How long will the shadows of houses oppress you? How long will the smoky prison of these cities close you in? Believe me, I behold a little more light."

This moving appeal touches the heart of the reader and serves to reveal very clearly Jerome's high purpose to serve God in the solitude of the desert. It makes very clear also his need of friendship and companionship.

While he lived in the desert of Chalcis Jerome wrote his biography of Paul of Thebes. He sent it to another Paul, the centenarian of Concordia, which is near Aquileia. Here, too, he composed his first commentary on the prophet Obadiah, which is no longer extant. As this latter work is not mentioned in the list of his writings contained in Jerome's book on Christian authors, it is quite possible that he himself decided in later years that the book was not worth preserving.

Jerome records that he earned his bread by the sweat

of his brow, but we are not informed as to the nature of his labors. Work would certainly be helpful to a lonely man. That he was not entirely alone seems evident from the fact that he had pupils, who were learning how to copy old books. We know that he supplemented his personal library by borrowing books. The aged Paul sent him books from Concordia, and Florentinus sent him books from Jerusalem.

To Florentinus Jerome wrote: "I request that you have transcribed on papyrus by the hand of your copyist those books which the brief enclosure will indicate that I do not have." The list has not survived, though the letter has. Jerome asks also for a copy of a translation of the Psalms "and that very profuse book on the synods by St. Hilary, which I transcribed with my own hand at Trier." Possibly he had lent his own manuscript to his friend and now wished to have it back. Jerome also offers to lend Florentinus such books of his own as he may desire.

Jerome studied Hebrew while in the desert under a reputed Chaldean Jew or convert to Christianity. This teacher helped him also in exegesis, informing him how the Hebrews interpret the vision of Isaiah "in the year that King Uzziah died."

Having retired into the waste places of the earth to be alone, it came as somewhat of a shock to Jerome to find how densely the desert was populated by other hermits. They lived, for the most part, in caves among the rocks. Their chief occupation, he felt was passing judgment upon the world from the seclusion of their retreats. Many of them were hostile to him. Jerome's final verdict on what had once seemed to him a paradise is this: "It is better to dwell among wild beasts than with such Christians."

After five years in the desert — in the spring of 379 — Jerome asked to be ordained a priest, but only on the express condition that he be permitted to remain a monk. He had by now determined to leave the East and did not wish to be tied down to any one spot. So the desert experience came to an end.

It may be well to consider more fully some of the reasons for this. Fundamentally it was because Jerome had lost his peace of mind and heart.

CONTROVERSY IN THE DESERT

"What exile from home ever escapes from himself?" asked the Roman poet Horace in the days of Augustus. So Jerome, too, realized at last that he had changed only his geographical location — not the warfare within the spirit of man. In the last analysis it was theology that was principally instrumental in bringing Jerome back from his retreat in the desert to the busy world of men.

The first general council of the Church, held at Nicea in 325, had declared the Arians, the Unitarian group of the time, to be heretics. But the followers of Athanasius, the orthodox Christians, were by no means united. In Syria there were at this time three opposing parties, headed respectively by Meletius, Vitalis, and Paulinus, each of whom claimed to be the rightful bishop of Antioch. So also did Euzoios the Arian put in his claim.

This situation had its origin in 330, when Eustathius, the orthodox bishop, was deposed. A minority still claimed to be of his party. The priest Paulinus had succeeded Eustathius, and Athanasius recognized Paulinus and his adherents as the orthodox group.

As for Meletius, his tenure had been somewhat uncertain, to say the least, He had formerly been Bishop of Sebaste, in Armenia. In 360 he was selected as Bishop of Antioch in the actual presence of Constantius, the official head of the state, and was consecrated by the bishop of Caesarea. But within a month the Emperor deposed him and sent him back home. Euzoios, the Arian, succeeded him. Thereupon those who still upheld Meletius conducted their church services separately out of doors. Hence they became known as *Campenses:* "the church of Meletius in the Fields."

In 362 a synod presided over by Athanasius had tried to end the schism, demanding only explicit rejection of Arianism. On this occasion the party of Paulinus had been recognized as orthodox and directed to unite with that of Meletius, the *Campenses.* Meanwhile Julian had permitted Meletius to return to Antioch. He was naturally unwilling to make way for Paulinus who had more recently been consecrated as Bishop of Antioch. In general, the Western church supported Paulinus, the Eastern upheld Meletius.

When Valens became Caesar of the East he again afforded the Arians the official support of the court. But upon his death in 378, the Emperor Gratian sent Meletius back to Antioch as bishop.

There was a third party, smaller in numbers, headed by Apollinaris of Laodicea, who had been Jerome's teacher. When forced out of the Church for heretical views in 376,

probably in the spring of 379 that Jerome was ordained as
a priest by Paulinus.

FRIENDSHIP'S VICISSITUDES

But the five years from 374 to 379 had effected great
changes in Jerome's life. Stridon, his home town, must have
seemed to him too small and too backward a town in which
to live after his return from Rome. Trier, which he had
visited on his way back, though it was at the time the
center of government and power in the West, had appealed
to him still less. When he reached Aquileia, his emotional
life had for three years found satisfaction in companionship with the band of ascetics who were making that city
their temporary headquarters. Then they had scattered to
the four winds. Next came the desert experience. Of his
closest associates, Innocent was dead. Jerome's foster
brother Bonosus was a lonely hermit on an island in the
Adriatic. "Your Bonosus," says Jerome in an early letter to
Rufinus, "no, I mean mine and, to speak more accurately,
ours — is now climbing the ladder shown by a portent in
Jacob's dream. He is bearing his cross. He takes no thought
for the morrow. He does not look back. He is sowing in
tears that he may reap in joy. . . . Lo a young man, educated with us in the liberal arts, who had ample means,
high station among his peers, now setting at naught his
mother, his sisters, and the brother who was dearest to
him, like a new colonist of Paradise has settled upon an
island dangerous to ships because of the sea that roars
about it, whose sharp reefs and bare rocks and solitude

are a source of terror to him. No farmer is there, no monk, not even that tiny Onesimus whom you know, in whom he used to take delight as in a little brother. In so great a desolation no comrade is by his side."

Jerome continues, saying in a prayer to God for his foster brother Bonosus: "Thou knowest how he and I grew up together from tender infancy even to the flower of our age; how the bosom of the same nurses, the embraces of the same servants cherished us. And when — after our schooldays at Rome — we ate the same food and shared the same lodgings by the semi-barbarous banks of the Rhine, as I first began to wish to worship Thee, remember, I pray, how that warrior of Thine was once a raw recruit with me."

When he wrote this letter to Rufinus, Jerome had not yet entered the desert of Chalcis. For he says to God of Bonosus: "He has accomplished, while I only had the will; forgive me that I was unable to accomplish. Bestow upon him the reward he deserves."

We do not know that Jerome and Bonosus ever saw each other again. He prays to God: "Let not your mind — like our eyes — lose sight of a friend." And he continues: "For a friend, long sought, is rarely come upon, and is hard to keep. Anyone may shine resplendent with gold, and glittering metals may gleam from the trappings of showy litters; love cannot be purchased. Affection has no price. Friendship that can cease was never real."

There speaks the lonely exile, far from home and friends.

Rufinus had gone to Egypt. His love for this friend of his youth is shown in an early letter in which Jerome says: "If only our Lord Jesus Christ would suddenly grant me

the swift passage of Philip to the eunuch, or of Ambacus
(i.e., Habakkuk) to Daniel, how tightly I would clasp your
neck with my embraces! How I would imprint kisses upon
that mouth that has sometimes erred with me, and sometimes uttered wisdom. . . . I send to greet you in my stead
this letter, to lead you to me fast bound by the tie of love."

But their meeting was long delayed. After eight years
in Egypt, Rufinus went with his friend and patron Melania
to Jerusalem. Late in life the friendship of Jerome and
Rufinus was marred by a disagreement about theological
matters.

Heliodorus, on whose companionship in the desert Jerome
had counted, had changed his plans and was now a member
of the regular clergy. Niceas, too, had returned home.

There had been family troubles at home. Jerome's sister
had occasioned anxiety for a time by waywardness, but had
been rescued and was now apparently planning to devote
herself to the religious life. "My sister is the fruit in Christ
of the saintly Julian," writes Jerome. . . . "He restored her
to life from the dead. . . . You yourselves know how slippery
is the path of youth. . . . As she enters upon *this* path [the
reference now is to a new dedication of her life], she must
be sustained . . . by the encouragement of all." He says to
Chromatius, Jovinus and Eusebius, to whom this letter is
addressed: "She must be strengthened by frequent letters
emanating from your saintliness. . . . I beseech that you
obtain from Father Valerian also a letter to hearten her.
You know that a girl's courage is often made firm by the
knowledge that she is an object of concern to her elders."

Jerome had little confidence in Lupicinus, the priest in

his home town of Stridon. "A crippled pilot steers a leaky ship," he says. "And a blind guide leads the blind into a pit." To another friend, Deacon Julian of Aquileia, Jerome wrote: "I rejoice that I got word first from you that my sister, your daughter in Christ, is persisting in her undertaking."

Evagrius was the friend closest to Jerome while he lived in Syria. He was making himself known by letter to Pope Damasus. But, on the whole, his life in the desert was a lonely one, relieved by his studies and writings but rendered unhappy by the disappointment of seeing unworthy fellow monks in the desert. Finally there was the uncertainty occasioned by seeing so many claimants to the see of Antioch.

So the great dream of salvation by a retreat from the world for private meditation and prayer had come to an end. It appeared that Aristotle had been correct in his appraisal of man as a social being. At all events, Jerome had decided to go back into the world of men. We may perhaps assume that he had found greater peace of mind once he had decided to support Paulinus, and had been ordained by him to the priesthood.

It appears that, upon forsaking the desert, Jerome lived for a time in Antioch until the Second Council of the Church, held in 381, at Constantinople. In company with Bishop Paulinus he attended this council. Upon his arrival in New Rome on the Bosphorus he found Gregory of Nazianzus ruling over the churches of that city. We know it best under the name Constantinople. However, it was earlier called Byzantium, and is at present known by the

Greek phrase that signifies "to the City" — *Istanbul*. The great church of Holy Wisdom had not yet been erected at this time. But the importance of its site had from the beginning predestined the city that was founded on the Bosphorus to be significant in world history. Jerome probably visited the Symplegades or "twin-clashing rocks" — the low headlands that face each other at the point where the narrow strait pours forth from the Black Sea. Doubtless he recalled the tale of Jason and the Argonauts, and of Medea, whom the Greek hero met there. While Jerome never mentions explicitly the Council of 381, he does make an incidental allusion to Gregory of Nyssa, a brother of Basil the Great, who attended it.

In general, the Council must have been distasteful to him as it was presided over by Meletius until his sudden death. Then Gregory of Nazianzus became its presiding officer. He proposed making Paulinus bishop of Antioch, but was so bitterly opposed that Gregory resigned the chair and left Constantinople. Thereupon Flavian succeeded Meletius (as bishop of Antioch) with Antioch's approval, though the West continued to uphold Paulinus.

While at Constantinople Jerome studied exegesis under Gregory of Nazianzus. Jerome relates an amusing incident about him. He says that when he asked his teacher to explain the meaning of the expression "second first sabbath," Gregory replied jestingly: "I'll tell you about that in church. There while all the people acclaim me you will be forced against your will to know what you do not know, or else, if you alone keep silence, you will be accounted the only fool present!" Gregory, too, was an advocate of celibacy, and had written a poem in hexameters in praise of virginity.

One important consequence of their meeting was that Gregory directed Jerome's attention to Origen, the greatest theologian of the Greek Church, and persuaded him to translate his writings into Latin.

Thus we see that Jerome's earliest work of translation consisted of Latin versions of the Greek fathers of the Church. Jerome had already translated 14 of Origen's homilies, including those on Isaias (Isaiah), Jeremias (Jeremiah), and Ezechiel (Ezekiel).

In the summer of 382 Jerome accepted an invitation from Pope Damasus to attend a synod at Rome. Jerome made the journey in company with his friend Bishop Paulinus, and Bishop Epiphanius of Salamis in Cyprus.

BACK TO ROME AGAIN: 382–385

This three year period marks a new and unique phase of Jerome's interesting and varied career. He was now back in the world's capital — the most famous city on earth. Of necessity he mingled with the society of the day. He met and became closely associated with Pope Damasus, who induced him to undertake the important task of revising the Latin text of the Psalms and the New Testament.

Now Jerome was frequently in the company of noble ladies: Paula, the heiress of the great Aemilian family and her two daughters, Blesilla and Eustochium; and the wealthy Marcella. At the latter's palace on the Aventine Hill Jerome and his pupils used to meet for the study of Hebrew and to hold prayer meetings. Moved by his teaching and example, these society leaders declared themselves ready to forsake the luxury and the splendor of Rome and to follow the ascetic life. Jerome himself sums it up for us in a famous letter. He says: "For almost three years I lived with them. Often a great crowd of young girls surrounded me. To some I often lectured on Scripture to the best of my ability. Our study brought about familiarity, familiarity friendship, and friendship created confidence."

Jerome was probably happier here than he had ever been before in his life. He was a born teacher, and missionary work appealed to him particularly. Moreover, he loved association with other people. How great a contrast was this with his former lonely hermit existence! He was now a person of prominence in a great metropolis.

But disaster struck suddenly and Jerome's position changed almost overnight. Four months after her baptism Blesilla, formerly a gay young widow, fell ill and died. In the enthusiasm of recent conversion, she had plunged with abandon into the austerities which Jerome himself practiced and which he recommended to others. People were quick to believe that her illness and death were to be attributed to the fasting and asceticism he had advocated. Jerome himself tells how weak she became from fasting, and speaks of her suffering for thirty days from fever. After Blesilla's death, which plunged both her mother and Jerome himself into deep sorrow, Jerome wrote a memorial letter, addressed to Paula. "This whole book is written with my tears," he says. He records Blesilla's touching last words: "Pray the Lord Jesus to forgive me because I was unable to perform what I wanted to do." Jerome declares that she shall henceforth become the theme of his writings: "Not a page shall fail to speak of Blesilla." An eternal remembrance is to compensate for the brief span of her earthly life. "In my books," he says, "she shall never die."

The high feeling caused by Blesilla's death gave rise to widespread indignation. Jerome was called "the Greek" and "the impostor." He was stoned for the letter he had written to Eustochium, Blesilla's sister, on the ascetic life. Now false and scandalous charges were brought against him, accusations later retracted and shown to have been groundless. Jerome could scarcely comprehend the sudden shift in public opinion. Conscious of his innocence, he was amazed at the things now said of him. "I a scandal, a turncoat, a slippery charlatan, I a liar, deceiving people by Satan's art!" He declares that some of those who kissed his hands maligned him behind his back. Now "their lips lamented" — at his downfall — "their hearts rejoiced." It is always difficult for a sincere and upright man to be convinced that hypocrites actually exist. His unconscious gestures, and even his walk and laugh, were now criticized. At this crisis in his life, Pope Damasus died, and Jerome — who had hoped perhaps to succeed him — was not chosen to head the Roman Church. Instead he was forced to go into exile. "I write this in haste," he says in his farewell letter, "grieving and in tears," and he adds: "They have burdened me with the disgrace of a false accusation, but I know that one attains to the kingdom of heaven through good report and through evil report." His comfort is in the fact that there is justice in the end: "We shall stand before the judgment-seat of Christ."

In 385 Jerome took ship and left Rome and Europe forever. "Do you want to know my itinerary when I left the City?" Jerome inquires of his friend Rufinus in a later writing. "I'll tell it to you briefly. It was in the month of August, and the etesian winds were blowing. I embarked in full confidence at the port of Rome with the holy priest Vincentius and my young brother [Paulinian — perhaps pursuing his studies in Rome at the time] and other monks who now dwell in Jerusalem. A great crowd of my friends among the clergy saw me off."

He reached Rhegium and stood for a time at the very spot familiar to him from his schooldays as the place where crafty Ulysses had encountered Scylla and Charybdis, and also at the spot where he had heard the Sirens' song.

While staying there he was advised by inhabitants of Sicily not to make for Africa but rather for Joppa — whence Jonah had set sail for Tarshish (possibly in Spain). But Jerome says that he chose to go by way of the Malean promontory of Greece and the Cyclades, and so to the island of Cyprus, where he was welcomed and entertained by the venerable Bishop Epiphanius of Salamis. Jerome must have recalled his Horace and the legend of the founding of Salamis after the Trojan War by Teucer, unwilling to face his father since his brother Ajax, entrusted to his charge, had committed suicide. Jerome doubtless, too, quoted the familiar lines of the Venusian bard — so appropriate now to his own case: "O brave men, you who have often suffered worse trials with me, let us now dispel our cares with wine. Tomorrow we shall sail onward across the mighty deep."

His next stop was at Antioch, where he enjoyed reunion with his confessor, Bishop Paulinus. After the arrival of Paula and Eustochium, the bishop escorted Jerome and his party to Jerusalem. "There I saw many wonderful sights," says Jerome, "and what I had previously known only by hearsay I verified by the judgment of my eyes." In the memorial to Paula written after her death, Jerome gives their itinerary in detail.

"Then I hastened on my way to Egypt," he continues; whether by the land route or by sea we do not know. "I beheld the monasteries of Nitria" (not far from Alexandria), he says, "and perceived that serpents are lurking amid the companies of the saints." Here, too, it appears, hypocrisy was to be found!

He hastened back to Bethlehem to worship at the place of Jesus' birth. "I also saw that most renowned lake [the Sea of Galilee], nor did I give myself over to mere idleness, but I learned many things of which I was ignorant before."

Not long after Jerome's departure, his friends, Paula and her daughter, had also forsaken Italy for the East. Jerome gives a touching picture of their departure and of the friends and relatives who stood on the shore at Ostia bidding them a last sad farewell. Her little son Toxotius held out suppliant hands. Her young daughter Rufina, now of marriageable age, said nothing — but her sobs were eloquent. Another daughter, Paulina, was the wife of Jerome's friend Pammachius at Rome.

Paula and Eustochium went first to Antioch, where Jerome joined them. They then journeyed together to Jerusalem and then to Egypt.

CHAPTER IV · TRAVELS IN THE HOLY LAND

ST. JEROME was blessed with loyal friends as long as he lived. When he was forced to flee from Rome in 385, Paula and Eustochium were two of his companions. To be sure, Paula's decision to follow Jerome was not made impulsively. Ever since she had entertained Bishop Epiphanius of Salamis in Cyprus ("which is now called Constantia," says Jerome) in 382, Paula had been strongly tempted to visit the Holy Land and the pioneer hermits of Egypt — men like Anthony and Paul, whose biographies were written by Jerome — and perhaps even to enter a convent there, even though this would involve forsaking her younger children at Rome. Thirteen years earlier, in 372, the wealthy widow Melania had left Rome and her only child for the East, having as an associate on her travels in Egypt and Palestine Jerome's boyhood friend Rufinus. Melania had founded a convent on the Mount of Olives in Jerusalem. Here was a precedent that Jerome may have pointed out to Paula.

At all events Paula and Eustochium left Rome a few months after Jerome's departure, in 385. Jerome gives us their itinerary in a memorial letter written after Paula's death. Paula and Eustochium landed first on the island of Pontia, where the Roman emperor Domitian's niece, Flavia Domitilla, had suffered martyrdom for her Christian faith.

At Methone in Greece they again stopped to rest. Proceeding then by way of the Cyclades — and Jerome quotes an
appropriate passage from Vergil to indicate their course —
they came to the island of Rhodes, then to Lycia in Asia
Minor, and finally to the island of Cyprus, one of Paula's
chief objectives. There she visited the venerable Epiphanius,
who invited her to stay and rest. However, she spent ten
days there not for rest, but in visiting the monasteries on the
island. On her departure, Paula left gifts for the brethren
there.

Then she sailed to Seleucia, in Asia Minor, and thence
proceeded by land to Antioch. Now in midwinter, this noble
lady, in her burning zeal, once accustomed to be carried
by eunuchs in a litter, made her arrival riding on a donkey.

Jerome lists the places, familiar to all Biblical students,
which she now visited in company with Bishop Paulinus
and Jerome. Many historical and mythological sites were
pointed out to them in the course of their travels. There
was the Roman colony of Berytus, known today as Beirut;
the ruins of Sidon (to which they went because Jesus, too,
had visited the coasts of Tyre and Sidon); and, at Sarepta,
the Zarephath of the Old Testament, a little tower associated with the story of Elias (Elijah). At Tyre they prayed
to God on the beach where Paul had fallen upon his knees
("we kneeled down on the shore, and prayed," says Luke
in The Acts). So they came to Acre, or Acco, also known
as Ptolemais, and destined in later centuries to be the
Crusaders' stronghold. Then they visited the battlefield of
Megiddo, where King Josiah died in 609 B.C.

Coming next to the land of the Philistines, they marveled

Statue of St. Jerome in front of Bethlehem parish
church dedicated to St. Catherine of Alexandria.
The four bronze doors of the church bear the
figures of Paula, Jerome, Eusebius, and Eustochium.

Entrance to the Church of the Nativity in Bethlehem,
through which one may reach the birthplace of our Lord and the
adjacent cell of St. Jerome.

A close-up of the small doorway, which was substituted for the larger
opening to keep infidel horsemen out of the church.

at the ruins of the once mighty city of Dor and a place
called (says Jerome) Strato's Tower, renamed Caesarea by
Herod, king of Judaea, in honor of Caesar Augustus. Here
they visited a church on the site of the home of Cornelius,
the Roman centurion. Luke relates that this soldier fell
down at Peter's feet but was raised up and told by the
apostle: "Get up, I myself also am a man." It was here
that the gift of the Holy Spirit was poured out upon the
Gentiles. They also visited the house of Philip the evangelist
and the chamber of his four virgin daughters, who had the
gift of prophecy. The house was now a Christian church.

The modern visitor to the Holy Land is impressed by
the fact that churches have been erected over practically
all the ancient sacred places.

They discovered the partially ruined town of Antipatris,
where Paul was taken by night, to save his life, by soldiers
charged by the tribune Claudius Lysias to conduct him in
safety to Caesarea, to Governor Felix. Antipatris was thus
named, says Jerome, by Herod in honor of his father
Antipas. At Lydda, then called Diospolis, they were reminded of the miraculous healing of Aeneas; at Joppa of
the raising of Tabitha (Dorcas) from the dead by the
Apostle Peter. Not far away was the village of Arimathea,
the home of that Joseph who provided for the Lord's burial
his own new tomb in Jerusalem. Arimathea is the ancient
Ramah, where Deborah, the prophetess and judge of Israel,
dwelt under a palm tree, and where Samuel the judge once
had his house.

"Nob," says Jerome, "once a city of priests, consists now
of the tombs of the slain." Here Samuel ate the hallowed

loaves known as the shewbread, as related in the first book of Kings (Samuel). The priests were afterward slain by King Saul because they were adherents of David.

The confusing thing about a pilgrimage to so ancient a land as Palestine — Lebanon, Syria, Israel, and Jordan today — is that it contains memorials of events covering not centuries but millennia of time. On the cliffs above the Dog River in Lebanon, for example, the only pass by which this country can be entered from the north, are to be read inscriptions in Egyptian, Assyrian, Greek, Latin, French, and English. They emphasize the shortness of the time that any nation can by mere force of arms rule over even a small spot of earth.

At Joppa, the modern Jaffa, they were reminded both of Jonah (who set sail from this port for Tarshish, in disobedience to God's command that he should go to Nineveh), and also of the fable of Perseus and Andromeda. Here they saw the very rock to which the maiden was chained to be the prey of the sea monster. Next they visited Nicopolis, known in the New Testament as Emmaus, where the risen Jesus was revealed to two of His disciples in the breaking of the bread. There, we are told, Paula dedicated the house of Cleopas as a church.

From Emmaus they made their way to Upper and Nether Beth-horon, cities founded by King Solomon. To their right, as they approached the vicinity of Jerusalem, they caught a glimpse of Aijalon and Gibeon, where Joshua the son of Nun fought victoriously against five kings, causing both the sun and the moon to stand still until the carnage was complete.

"Leaving on the left the mausoleum of Helena, the queen of the Adiabeni who had helped the people with grain in time of famine, they entered Jerusalem, the city of three names: Jebus, Salem, and Jerusalem" (i.e., "Holy Salem"). Jerusalem, of course, was one of the chief objectives of their tour.

JERUSALEM AND GALILEE

"If I forget you, O Jerusalem, may my right hand be forgotten!" said the Psalmist of old. The Holy City is still a chief object of veneration for Jew, Christian, and Moslem alike. Jerome tells us of Paula's emotion upon seeing it. The Roman governor of Palestine at that time was a close friend of her family, and he did all in his power to make her stay a comfortable one. But she selected a humble cell as her home, and gave herself enthusiastically to sight-seeing. To her it was all holy ground, and she could scarcely be torn away from the first places she visited; yet she was in haste to see all the rest! She prostrated herself before the cross, discovered by St. Helena on May 3, 326, and seemed to see the Lord suffering upon it. She entered the sepulcher of Christ's burial and resurrection, and kissed the stone which the angel had rolled away from the door of the tomb, and the place where the Lord's body had lain. Jerome says: "What tears she wept there, what mournful groanings she uttered, all Jerusalem can bear witness." Upon going forth from that place she ascended Mt. Zion.

Jerome quotes from the eighty-sixth Psalm (1–2): "His foundation upon the holy mountains the Lord loves: the gates of Sion, more than any dwelling of Jacob," and then he says: "Not those gates which we see today reduced to ruin and ashes, but the gates against which hell does not prevail, and through which the multitude of believers enters into the presence of Christ."

In Jerusalem there was pointed out a column supporting a portico of the church, stained with the blood of the Lord, to which He is said to have been bound when He was scourged. The pilgrims were also shown the room where the Holy Spirit descended upon a hundred and twenty persons.

After Jerusalem the little party proceeded to Bethlehem, passing the tomb of Rachel on the way. There in the birthplace of Jesus, Jerome tells us: "In my hearing she [Paula] swore that she could see with the eyes of faith the infant wrapped in swaddling bands crying in the manger; the magi worshipping God; the star shining down from above; the virgin mother, a devoted nurse; the shepherds coming by night . . . the slain children; Herod raging and Joseph and Mary fleeing into Egypt."

After Bethlehem, Jerome and his friends set out on the old road to Gaza. They came to Beth-zur and after that to Eshcol — named from the bunch of grapes which it took two men to carry, a direct reference to the days of Moses.

Then they came to Hebron in ancient Canaan, where they saw traces of Abraham's Oak at Mamre, and the memorials of Sarah, his wife, and of Isaac.

Oddly Jerome declares that Paula was unwilling to go to Kirjath-sepher, "the City of Letters," because "despising the letter that killeth, she had found the spirit that giveth life." She marveled at "the upper and the nether watery ground," which Othniel the son of Cenez had received in place of the dry southern country — an irrigated land. Jerome sees in this an analogy with the sacrament of baptism whereby man's sins are taken away.

They looked down upon the broad expanse of wasteland where Sodom and Gomorrha had once stood before they were destroyed by the Lord for their wickedness "burning it with brimstone, and the heat of salt, so that it cannot be sown any more, nor any green thing grow therein." This country, adjacent to the Dead Sea, when seen today from an airplane, seems desolate indeed.

Realizing how he had digressed from his main purpose of extolling Paula in his scholarly interest in the ancient sites mentioned in the books of Moses, Jerome says: "I shall return to Jerusalem" (by way of Tekoa, with its memories of Amos, and the Mount of Olives, from which Jesus ascended into heaven). On the way they visited the tomb of Lazarus and saw the house of Mary and Martha at Bethany. Then they went down to Jericho (where "The Inn of the Good Samaritan" is still pointed out today). There they saw the sycamore tree climbed by Zaccheus that he might see Jesus passing by, and the spot where two blind men had sat and besought the Lord to have mercy upon them.

Strange how in all ages of the Church men have tried to identify and to mark out for posterity each slightest spot connected with the Gospel and with the life of Jesus. And we should remember that much of this ancient biblical history is interwoven with pious tradition.

Jerome, the scholar and archaeologist, calls attention to

the fact that Jericho was built by Hiel: "he laid the foundation thereof in Abiram his first-born, and set up the gates thereof in his youngest son Segub" — as had been prophesied by Joshua at the time that he destroyed the earlier city and forbade its rebuilding. That is, the sacrifice of his children was a necessary prerequisite to the rebuilding.

Excavations now in progress at Jericho have revealed the world's oldest walled city, whose founding has been estimated at 5000 B.C., in the middle bronze age. This, then, was a predecessor of that city whose walls fell flat when the Israelites under Joshua blew their trumpets: "and every man went up by the place that was over against him: and they took the city."

They saw Gilgal, the place of the second wholesale circumcision; and the twelve stones carried by Joshua's command by representatives of the twelve tribes, every man carrying a stone upon his shoulder. These were set down in the midst of Jordan that the priests who bore the ark might cross over on dry land. Jerome sees in these stones a symbol of the twelve apostles. They also visited the spring which Elisha miraculously "healed": "there shall be no more in them death or barrenness."

"It would take too long," says Jerome, "were I to speak of the valley of Achor [where Achan and his family, and even his cattle, were stoned and afterward burned because of Achan's disobedience to the Lord's command], and of Bethel, 'the house of God,' where Jacob slept, with a stone for a pillow, and saw in a dream the ladder whose top reached to heaven, with 'the angels of God ascending and descending on it.'" They also venerated the tomb of Joshua "in mount Ephraim, on the north side of mount Gaas." There they visited the grave of Eleazar, the son of Aaron. Here (says Jerome) Paula wondered that a distributor of possessions (she means Joshua) had chosen for himself mountainous and rugged country! There speaks the low-lander, accustomed to no eminence greater than the seven hills of Rome.

Then they proceeded to Shechem (now called Neapolis, says Jerome) in Samaria, "and entered the church erected above Jacob's Well, on the slopes of Mt. Gerizim" — where Jesus spoke to the woman of Samaria.

Jacob's Well is one of the few absolutely authentic sites in the Holy Land. The well, still in use today, is in the crypt of the church, and is accessible by two flights of stairs, one used for those descending and the other to be used as an exit.

They went on to Sebaste, the ancient Samaria, now called Nablus, with its memories of Omri the father of Ahab, Jezebel's husband. Here one may still see a Jewish wall that dates back to the eighth century B.C. In the first century Herod the Great built a Roman temple on the site of Ahab's ivory palace which may still have been in fair condition when Jerome and his friends visited Sebaste. That was the Greek word equivalent to the Latin *Augustus*, and Herod called ancient Samaria by this name in honor of the first Roman emperor.

Here the pilgrims must have visited the grave of John the Baptist: that is, the grave of his body. His head, oddly enough, is buried in the Ommiad mosque in Damascus.

Proceeding farther north, they came to Nazareth, Cana

and Capharnaum — all on or near the Sea of Galilee. These once populous cities have all disappeared, even as Jesus prophesied, referring to Chorazin, Bethsaida, and Capharnaum by name.

The most impressive thing to be seen at Capharnaum today is a little white temple: four columns supporting a broken architrave remain standing. Many architectural fragments are to be seen adjacent to it, along a country road. These are the ruins of an ancient synagogue — perhaps the very one in which Jesus preached. At all events this shore is the region where Peter lived, and where the Lord first saw Simon and Andrew and James and John.

In Cana of Galilee there is a church erected on the site of the house where Jesus turned water into wine at a wedding feast — His first miracle.

In our visit, we came down from a steep hill into Nazareth just at dusk, and were at once aware of an incongruity that did not yet exist in Jerome's time. For we heard a muezzin proclaiming from his slender tower the call to prayer that may be heard, in Arabic, everywhere in the Moslem lands. At the same time there was the sound of chanting in Latin from the Roman Catholic Church. Nearby, pupils in a Jewish school were repeating their lessons in unison — aloud — in Hebrew. And from a restaurant across the street there proceeded strains of American jazz music, via radio. Truly a confusion of tongues!

We, too, saw the spring — the only one in the village — to which Mary doubtless used to come to draw water. The site is authentic. We visited the Franciscan church — a religious order founded almost a thousand years after

Jerome's visit to Nazareth — erected where the Holy Family lived in a cave or grotto after their return from Egypt. Joseph's workshop is pointed out to the modern visitor above the baptismal font of the Byzantine Church. And there is, also, "the Church of the Synagogue" commemorating the spot where Jesus spoke, saying: "This day is fulfilled this scripture in your ears." Not far distant is the "Mount of the Precipitation" ("the brow of the hill") from which his angry fellow townsmen proposed to throw him down headlong, "But he, passing through the midst of them, went his way."

Cana and Capharnaum were considered holy by Jerome because of the miracles performed there. "For if the miracles had been worked in Sodom that have been worked in thee," said Jesus, apostrophizing Capharnaum, "it had remained to this day."

The Sea of Galilee was consecrated, to the mind of Jerome, by the fact that our Lord sailed upon it.

Much, of course, has changed in the course of the centuries. But Jerome and Paula could behold the natural features of the land where Jesus once lived, its hills and fields, its river and its seas, and could say: Jesus once walked on this soil and lifted up His eyes to these very hills.

FURTHER TRAVELS IN THE HOLY LAND AND IN EGYPT

Jerome records the fact that Paula climbed Tabor, the Mount of the Transfiguration, not far from Nazareth, which is a beautifully rounded eminence rising not more than 1900 feet above sea level, and visible for a great distance across the plain of Esdraelon. Matthew's Gospel calls it "a high mountain apart," as there are no other hills near it. While Jerome does not say that he also climbed to the summit, it seems reasonable to assume that he did. He goes on to say: "She saw far off Mt. Hermon," that is, the range on the border of Israel and Lebanon, whose snow-capped ridge is a landmark as one flies from Cairo to Beirut. Mt. Hermon rises to a height of 9166 feet above sea level, hence many Biblical scholars declare that the Transfiguration more probably took place on the slopes of this mountain — not on the relatively low Mt. Thabor.

However that may be, it is possible to get a memorable view from the summit of Thabor over a land famous in Biblical history. For here Sisera and his entire army were destroyed by Barak and Deborah. The river Kishon flows through the plain of Jezreel, and nearby is the little town of Naim, where Jesus raised from the dead "the only son of his mother, and she was a widow."

"The daylight will fail before my narrative ends," says Jerome, "if I wish to recount all that the venerable Paula explored, with faith beyond belief."

"I shall pass on to Egypt," he says, "and stand for a little while in Succoth and refresh my dry mouth at the fountain of Samson, which he produced from a tooth in the jawbone of an ass." Thus refreshed (he says) he will be able to see at Moreseth what was once the tomb of Micah and is now a church. This prophet uttered what has been called the greatest teaching of the Old Testament: "What the Lord requires of thee [is] verily to do judgment, and to love mercy, and to walk solicitous with thy God."

"I shall leave to one side," he says, recalling the journey he took with his friend many years before, when they first came to the Holy Land, "Idumea (the ancient Edom), and through the yielding sand that swallows up men's footprints and the vast unending desert, I shall come to the river of Egypt, the Sior, which is by interpretation 'turbid.' " Jerome goes on to mention the land of Goshen and the five cities of Egypt in which Canaanitish speech is used. And so they came to the port city of Alexandria.

It is interesting to speculate whether the pilgrims also visited en route the pyramids of Gizeh and the Sphinx, remembering the flight of the Holy Family into Egypt. But their chief reason for going to Egypt appears to have been to visit Nitria, "the Lord's town, wherein daily the guilty stains of many are most purely washed away by the natron of the virtues." There they met Bishop Isidore and "a countless throng" of monks; these latter had their cells in the desert outside of Nitria. "Whose cell did Paula not enter?" asks Jerome rhetorically; "at whose feet did she not cast herself? She believed that in the individual saints she was seeing Christ, and rejoiced that whatever she bestowed upon them she had bestowed upon the Lord." He says that forgetting her sex and bodily frailty, she longed to live with her young girls, the nuns, among so many thousand monks! But her desire for holier surroundings than the Sahara desert prevailed over this temporary whim. So she returned to Palestine with such speed that (says Jerome) "you might have supposed that she was a bird!"

"Not long afterward," he continues, "Paula took up her residence in Holy Bethlehem [where she was to remain for the rest of her life] for three years in crowded quarters, until she could erect cells and monasteries, and an inn near the road for pilgrims." The inn was included, says Jerome, "because Mary and Joseph had found no shelter."

The expenses of the enterprise were borne out of Paula's great wealth, and, after that was exhausted, by the proceeds of Jerome's inheritance.

In his long epistolary biographical sketch of Paula, Jerome pays tribute to this remarkable woman who renounced the world after the death of her husband, Julius Toxotius, saying: "No mind was more teachable than hers." And, in his fondness for nautical expressions, Jerome declares in a strikingly modern-sounding phrase that his account "goes on the rocks" when he tries to speak of her death. "Though every member of my body were transformed into a tongue, and every joint gave forth a human voice, I could say nothing worthy of the virtues of the saintly and venerable Paula." But it is his life, not hers, that we are here trying to portray.

Perhaps it has become evident that this ascetic, this monk, this solitary, was a human being whose nature craved friendship and affection. Surely the very number of his letters — 150 of them are extant — gives evidence of that fact.

But he sought human fellowship and companionship in daily intercourse with others as well as by letters. In later years, writing from Bethlehem to his friend Marcella at Rome, he says — to excuse the shortness of his letter: "I can't refuse to see the friends who have flocked to our little hostelry."

In the list of his writings Jerome states that he cannot

count his letters to Paula and Eustochium, because he wrote to them every day. The majority of these letters are concerned with the elucidation of Scriptural or theological points, and are quite impersonal. Nevertheless, they bear witness to his need of companionship, if only by the interchange of ideas in writing.

At the request of another friend, Fabiola, Jerome wrote his monographs about the vestments worn by Jewish priests, and the places which the Hebrews passed on their way to the Promised Land. Fabiola, too, visited the Holy Land and was staying with Jerome at the time the Huns invaded Palestine.

When criticized for writing so many letters to women, he defends himself by saying: "If it was no disgrace for the apostle to be taught by a woman [he is referring to the fact that Apollos was taught by Priscilla, as related by Luke in the book of The Acts], why should it be disgraceful for me, after teaching men, to teach women also?"

Jerome frequently wrote to people he had never met, and he even refers to the joy of an unexpected letter from a dear friend "on whom I had never set my eyes."

It is evident, then, that the years he spent at Bethlehem were far less lonely than those in the desert of Chalcis. For now he was surrounded by devoted friends and visited by many who looked upon him as a great and holy man. Moreover, he now had a definite task: that of making a new Latin translation of the Bible from the original Hebrew and Greek manuscripts, and writing commentaries to explain what it all meant.

But the extensive travels which he had first made in the

Holy Land had prepared him to write with fuller understanding of the places associated with the preaching and
teaching of Jesus, and the heroes of the Old Testament.
He had journeyed from Dan to Beersheba, and from the
Great Sea to the river Jordan. When he read of the man
who went down from Jerusalem to Jericho (from the Jerusalem ridge to a location eight hundred feet below sea
level) he could recall making that same descent himself.
He had probably stood beside the Jordan at the ford where
(according to the writer of the Old Testament book of
Judges) 42,000 of the Ephraimites were slaughtered by the
Gileadites because their speech betrayed them as an alien
stock.

How often in conversation with friends in later life, as
mention of some famous spot was made — Emmaus, or
Capharnaum, or the Mount of Olives — Jerome must have
answered with inner satisfaction: "I've been there!", for
this hermit had also been a great traveler.

CHAPTER V - EARLIER WRITINGS
IN ROME

So BEGINS the long final phase of Jerome's varied life, the time of his deepest happiness and finest achievement: a period devoted primarily to scholarship.

To review briefly what he had written before he forsook Rome for the East, his earliest works before he left Chalcis and Antioch for the West consisted of: a translation into Latin of Origen's homilies on Jeremias (Jeremiah), Ezechiel (Ezekiel), and Isaias (Isaiah), written between 379 and 381; his translation of the *Chronicle*, or *World History*, by Eusebius and his continuation of the record date from 325 to 378. This is not only intrinsically valuable, but has the added distinction of having served as a model for the annals of subsequent chroniclers of the Middle Ages. This work and his life of Paul, the first solitary, or hermit, date from the years in the desert, 374–379.

A second period of literary activity begins with his three year stay in Rome (382–385). At the suggestion of Pope Damasus, Jerome undertook, in 384, a correction of the Latin version of the Gospels, and then of the Epistles of St. Paul. Turning from this to the Old Testament, he made his first revision of the Latin Psalms according to the accepted pre-Christian Greek version of the Old Testament, known as the Septuagint. This revision is known as the Roman Psalter. Next he revised the Latin translation of Job according to the text of the Septuagint. All this was done in the year 384.

Jerome's second revision of the Psalter according to the sixfold text of Origen — the hexapla — falls in the years 386–391. This is the so-called "Gallican Psalter," incorporated in the Vulgate version of the Bible. The hexapla, an amazing piece of scholarly work, consists of six parallel columns. In the first is contained the Hebrew text in the original Hebrew characters; in the second the Hebrew text transliterated in the Greek alphabet. The third column contains the Greek translation of Aquila; the fourth that of Symmachus; the fifth the Septuagint version; and the sixth the version of Theodotion.

The Gallican Psalter is so called because it was first extensively used in Gaul.

While he was still in Rome, in fact in the first years of his stay (382–383), Jerome wrote the first of his polemical works: "A controversy between a follower of Lucifer and an orthodox Christian." This work is in the form of a dialogue between Helladius, a supporter of Lucifer of Cagliari, in Sardinia, and a representative of the orthodox Christian faith, and contains an account of the Council of Rimini to indicate the origin of this heterodox sect. The subject of discussion concerns what the attitude of the orthodox Church should be toward Arian Christians seeking admission to the Church: whether baptism previously administered by Arian priests shall be accepted as efficacious, and whether repentant Arian bishops may retain their ecclesiastical status.

Jerome supports the actual practice of the orthodox Church, which answered both questions in the affirmative. This is the only one of Jerome's polemical writings that is free from personalities.

At about the same time, while in Rome, Jerome wrote a treatise on the perpetual virginity of Mary, the mother of Christ, directed against Helvidius. The latter was a layman, a pupil of Auxentius, the Arian bishop of Milan, who had written a tractate in defense of the married state that was very disquieting to those who upheld ascetic practices and the celibate life. He declared that Joseph and Mary had children after the birth of Jesus who are referred to in Scripture as "his brethren." He based his belief on tradition as well as on the Gospels, and cited Tertullian and Victorinus in support of his position. Though Helvidius was not personally known to him, Jerome assumed an arrogant attitude and held him up to ridicule as "the only man in the world who is in his own person both layman and priest." This lack of objectivity and of restraint in language is to be deplored. But Jerome gloried in this rhetorical exuberance! So much for his earlier writings.

The first literary work at Bethlehem consists of his commentaries on four of the Epistles of St. Paul: Philemon, Colossians, and Ephesians (which he declares must all date from Paul's imprisonment in Rome), and Titus. He dedicated these commentaries to Paula and Eustochium.

Jerome's original intention had been to write commentaries on all of Paul's Epistles. He next undertook to compose one on Galatians, which proved to be one of his best. This work is notable for his attack on Marcion. He men-

tions several other gnostics and attacks Lactantius and
Chrysostom as well. He also assails Porphyrius, the keenest
antagonist of Christianity.

In these early exegetical works Jerome seems to waver
between historical and allegorical interpretation.

His explanations of the letter to the Ephesians show less
originality and are rather cursory. Here he draws heavily
on Origen and on his own teachers, Apollinaris and Didymus. In his prefaces he states that he wrote thousands of
lines daily. This excessive haste appears to have troubled
his conscience.

To be able to deal adequately with the Hebrew writings
of the Old Testament, Jerome now resumed his study of
Hebrew, which he had first undertaken while in the desert
of Chalcis. His teacher was a Jew named Baranina. To
avoid detection and possible criticism, he studied under him
by night. "How hard it was," he says — "and how expensive!"

The commentary on Ecclesiastes, his next project, is particularly valuable because it incorporates rabbinical inter-
pretations Jerome had learned from his teacher. Since he
had read this book with Blesilla in Rome, he now dedicated
the commentary to her memory.

At Bethlehem Jerome also began to devote himself to a
translation of the Old Testament from the original Hebrew.
But as it was an enormous task, he alternated this work
with a number of other writings for the sake of variety.

Three of his works written at this period of his life are
unique in Latin literature. The first is a lexicon of Hebrew
proper names, arranged by books of the Bible, and in al-
phabetical order under each book. It is essentially a trans-

lation of an earlier book in Greek by Eusebius. However, Jerome's work is extremely reliable because of his Hebrew scholarship. He makes corrections in the work of Eusebius on the basis of the Hebrew. This work is dated as having been written about 390 by the fact that Jerome mentions the capture of Nisibis by Lucullus and its recent recovery from the Persians by Jovian.

It is interesting to note that Jerome knows about Christian churches located in places mentioned in the Old Testament — although Eusebius does not. Jerome had seen them with his own eyes. Jerome also records the location of sacred relics. As might be expected, he shows a special knowledge of the antiquities of Bethlehem. This book by Jerome served to give the occidental Church a knowledge of the Holy Land, and was also a basis for a number of later guide books.

The second of these unique works is entitled "Hebrew Researches on Genesis." This philological inquiry into the original text is one of his best works. Jerome's purpose was to overcome the lack of confidence in the Hebrew text — as compared with the Septuagint. Jerome tries to amend the Latin version by comparing it with both the Hebrew and the Old Testament in Greek as cited by the Gospels and by St. Paul. This was preliminary to his own new translation of the Old Testament from the Hebrew.

The third of these works is a book dealing with Hebrew place names. The German scholar Grützmacher, who has written what is perhaps the best biography of Jerome, points out that the Assyrian, Babylonian, and Egyptian names necessarily included must have caused Jerome almost insuperable difficulties. He adds that perhaps even today no single individual is qualified to perform so tremendous a task. This particular work is evidence both of his scholarship and his courageous ambition in the fields of knowledge and instruction.

In the year 390 Jerome finally finished his translation of a work by Didymus on the Holy Spirit. Pope Damasus had asked him to compose a book on the Holy Spirit, but he preferred to make available in Latin the work of Didymus, under whom he had studied at Alexandria in Egypt. His version was so popular that it was generally preferred to the original. Consequently the original work has not come down to us.

In the preface to this translation Jerome bitterly attacks Bishop Ambrose of Milan — although he does not mention him by name. Ambrose had written a three volume treatise on the Holy Spirit which was not acceptable to Jerome. While at Rome, however, Jerome had spoken highly to Eustochium about a book on chastity written by Ambrose; and in his Chronicle, too, Jerome pays Ambrose a glowing tribute. Here, then, we have an instance of how Jerome sometimes separates in his mind the belief expressed from the person expressing it. But he attacks heretical opinions as such, regardless of the persons by whom they are held, and gives credit where credit is due.

FURTHER WRITINGS AT BETHLEHEM: 390–420

In the preface to his *Life of Malchus, the Captive Monk,* previously discussed, Jerome refers to a proposed history of the Church from the birth of Christ to his own time.

This work was to stress biographies, the human element in history, and thus show by whose instrumentality the Christian Church originated and grew. He was ahead of his age in realizing the importance of a study of great men. Indeed, it was not until 1920, at Carleton College, Northfield, Minnesota, that the first department of biography was founded in a modern institution of higher learning. Jerome's lives of Malchus and of Hilarion seem to have been first steps in the direction of such an ecclesiastical history. Hilarion holds the distinction of having established the monastic life in Palestine. Later he found in Cyprus the isolation and the peace of mind that he sought. He died there in 371. His name is still commemorated in Cyprus by St. Hilarion's Castle, a thirteenth century Gothic structure. This landmark, visited by tourists and archaeologists alike, stands some 2000 feet above the small town of Kyrenia.

The revision of the Latin New Testament text, undertaken at the request of Pope Damasus, was probably finished by 392. Thereupon Jerome turned his attention to the Old Testament and devoted about fifteen years to it. He completed this great piece of translation in 404.

His purpose in producing a new version was threefold. He wished to restore to the Bible parts that had been omitted in translation, and correct what was misinterpreted or lacking in clearness. Above all, he desired to set forth in clear and dependable speech what the Bible said.

In the year 383 Jerome had written to Pope Damasus; in his preface to the revision of the older Latin version of the four evangelists, he said: "It is a labor of love, yet it is also both dangerous and presumptuous, since in judging others I must consent to be judged by all. And how can I dare to change the world's language in its hoary old age, and restore it to the early days of its infancy?" This situation has confronted every translator of Scripture. But the scholar must strive to express clearly and at the same time as beautifully and impressively as he can, in the speech of his own time, what the ancient manuscripts contain. This may often involve abandoning a beautiful version of an earlier time, cherished because of its familiarity and because of the thousands who have committed it to memory, so that it seems the only authentic rendering.

Moreover, it is always difficult to express in modern language the ideas and ideals of an era separated from the translator's age and country by centuries or even millennia, and by racial as well as geographical differences. Jerome has the distinction of having hit the golden mean between the letter and the spirit. He wrote so as to be understood by his contemporaries.

When he began to translate the Old Testament from Hebrew into Latin, in 390, Jerome also started his series of commentaries on the prophetical books. He began with five of the minor prophets: Nahum, Micheas (Micah), Sophonias (Zephaniah), Aggeus (Haggai), Habacuc (Habakkuk). This task occupied the remainder of his life, and he left his commentary on Jeremiah unfinished when he died. In this work he was greatly helped by Origen's Greek commentaries. He says that in them he has the treasures of Croesus. Jerome explains not only his own new text, but also the Septuagint.

Nevertheless, it is from Hebrew tradition that Jerome de-rived his chronological data about the prophets. From the same source he obtained much historical, geographical, and philological matter. In general, he prefers the Hebrew text to the Septuagint — as might be expected. Sometimes he enlivens his commentaries from personal knowledge and experience. So, for example, he describes the Jews' mourning the destruction of the Temple as if he himself had witnessed it.

In 392 Jerome wrote one of his best known works, *On Famous Men*. The title is taken from a similar work written by Suetonius, the biographer of the twelve Caesars. Jerome's purpose was to refute the charge that the Christians were not a cultured people in the field of literature. "Let them stop accusing our people of a rustic simplicity," he says in his preface to the book.

This catalog of 135 Christian writers starts with Peter and ends with himself. In order to impress the pagans, Jerome includes heretical as well as orthodox writers, in this way increasing the total number of names. This was criticized by Augustine, who felt that Jerome ought at least to have called attention to their heterodoxy. But the last thing that Jerome wanted to do was to advertise differences of belief within the Christian Church. Starting with Arnobius in the second half of his work, Jerome becomes more subjective in his treatment. He does not include Augustine (who, at that time, had not yet written much) or his old school friend Rufinus.

During the seven year period from 385 to 392 we have only one letter addressed by Jerome to his friend Marcella in Rome. That it was written during the early days in

Bethlehem, perhaps in 386, seems clear from the fact that he still refers to Rome as "Babylon" and calls Jerusalem "Paradise." Ostensibly composed by Paula and Eustochium the letter was an invitation to come to Bethlehem: "The only thing we can do when absent from you is to pour forth complaining entreaties, and attest our longing for you not so much by sobs as by wailing, that you may restore our Marcella to us." And later in the letter we read: "O when shall that time come when a panting messenger shall bring us the news that our Marcella has reached the shore of Palestine?" But Marcella did not come.

In 390 Pope Siricius, who succeeded Damasus, had condemned the heresies of Jovinian. The latter's influence in Rome continued to be strong, however, and he had induced many to forsake the celibate life. Monastic ideals had never been as strong in the West as in the East. Paula's son-in-law, Pammachius, had written to Jerome, urging him to refute the heretic Jovinian. Jerome was always more than willing to speak or write in defense of virginity. In complying with his friend's request, in 392, he apparently overdid the matter. In consequence, Pammachius bought up and suppressed all the copies of Jerome's pamphlet against Jovinian! However, Jerome remarks — quoting from Horace: "A word once spoken cannot return!"

With his letter to Pammachius Jerome sent his translation of the sixteen books of the prophets and his commentaries on the twelve minor prophets. He also sent his commentary on the four books of Kings, which is no longer extant. He speaks of his translation of the book of Job, which he offers to borrow from Marcella so that Pammachius may read it.

When his wife Paulina died, Pammachius became a monk.

There was in Rome a devout descendant of the old Fabian gens, whose name was Fabiola. In her zeal for knowledge she had visited Palestine and met Jerome at Bethlehem. After she had returned home, Jerome wrote to her and sent her a monograph on the priestly vestments of the Jews, in which she had expressed an interest. After her death, in 399, he compiled and dedicated to her memory a work dealing with the places where the Israelites halted during their long wanderings in the wilderness. When she had questioned him about this on her visit to Bethlehem, Jerome had been embarrassed because he could not always give her the answers: "in many instances I simply confessed my ignorance," he says. But the matter troubled him, and he finally made the necessary study of Scripture and wrote this impressive little work, which emphasizes the thought that life is a pilgrimage, and explains allegorically the forty-two camps of the Israelites. "The time has come," he says, "to fulfill my promise, and recount in order the stopping-places of Israel." When he finished the work, Jerome sent it to Fabiola's relative Oceanus, one of his most influential friends at Rome.

In company with this Fabiola, Pammachius — after his wife's death — opened a hostel in Ostia, the port of Rome. "I hear," writes Jerome to him, "that you have built a guest-house in the port of Rome and planted on the shore of Ausonia a branch of Abraham's tree. . . . You are the first among the monks in the first city [of the world] first to follow the patriarch."

Mention has already been made of the fact that many of

Jerome's correspondents were not personally known to him. As a result, he often formed friendships with people whom he had never seen — "pen pals" they would perhaps have been called today! In 393, a native of Gaul whose name was Desiderius took the initiative in seeking Jerome's friendship. He wrote to ask Jerome to send him his works, and told him that he held the palm for eloquence. That made pleasant reading; but Jerome replied: "You know that my way of thinking upholds the standard of humility, and that by starting at the bottom we scale the heights." Jerome was greatly interested to learn that Desiderius and his sister, Serenilla, had both dedicated themselves to the religious life. Later, when Desiderius had become a priest in Aquitaine, Jerome invited him to undertake a pilgrimage to the Holy Land. He suggested that meanwhile he could use as an index to his writings the list published in the final chapter of his book "On Famous Men," and ask Jerome for whatever works he wished.

Somewhat earlier, in 375, Paulinus of Nola, born of a noble family in Bordeaux, had offered Jerome his friendship. This zealous man was to become bishop of Nola in 409. He was married, but both he and his wife had dedicated themselves to the religious life. After spending a few years in Spain they settled at Nola. There, at the grave of his favorite saint, Felix, he had erected a basilica and a hospital for monks and for the poor, reserving in this building modest quarters for himself and for his wife.

At a later time, when Paulinus expressed a desire to visit the Holy Land in order to make Jerome's acquaintance personally, Jerome tried to dissuade him, reminding him that places do not matter, and the true worshiper is he who is such in spirit and in truth — regardless of whether he be in Jerusalem or on Mt. Gerizim or elsewhere. "The true temple of Christ is the believer's soul," he says.

The reason for this attitude on Jerome's part is unknown to us. But the fact that Paulinus was able to maintain friendly relations with a number of Jerome's opponents, including Rufinus and Pelagius, may perhaps explain the situation. Paulinus was not greatly concerned about dogmas. Jerome was.

JEROME, THE CHRISTIAN ORACLE

As time went on and Jerome became more widely known through his writings, he began to be regarded as a Christian oracle. He was consulted about the meaning of Scripture and also on every sort of practical ecclesiastical or moral question.

For example, in one of his most interesting letters he writes to a mother and daughter living in Gaul and points out the dangers inherent even in friendship. "A certain brother from Gaul," says Jerome, "has informed me that he has an unmarried sister and a widowed mother, who live in the same city but in separate establishments. Either because of loneliness or to manage their property they have taken certain clergymen as advisers. This union with strangers has caused an even greater scandal than the fact of their separation from each other."

So, at the instigation of the young man who called on him in Bethlehem, Jerome (in 405) wrote to the two ladies in Gaul whom he had never met. To be sure, he sees the

unusual nature of the undertaking. "That's a fine task," he
says to the youth, "that you impose upon me, that I, a
stranger, should reconcile those whom a son and brother
has not been able to!" However he consented to try it. And
so he rebukes both mother and daughter in turn. He speaks
as if he actually saw the people to whom he is writing.
Anticipating the objection "How do you know — you're so
far away and have never set eyes on us," he replies: "Your
brother's tears and unendurable bursts of sobbing told me
this." And he adds: "Believe me, sister, no one weeps when
he is lying."

At the close he says: "I dictated this letter, speaking
rapidly, within one brief night." And he goes on to say:
"My tongue outstripped the speed of my secretaries' fingers."
Paula and Eustochium perhaps acted as his secretaries.

In a letter to a priest named Amandus, Jerome answers a
question about the meaning of certain Biblical passages and
also gives his opinion on remarriage after separation from
a former spouse. In reply to the latter inquiry, he calls attention to the saying of Jesus: "There are eunuchs who have
made themselves so for the kingdom of heaven's sake. Let
him accept it who can." This Amandus later became Bishop
of Burdigala.

A poet, Evangelus by name, wrote to ask about the priest
Melchisedech, the king of Salem who blessed Abram, and
who is referred to both in the Psalms and in the Epistle
to the Hebrews. In reply, he received a statement of what
Jerome had heard and read on the subject. At the close of
this letter Jerome states that he is recovering from a long
illness, a fever that continued for forty days. His eagerness

to write a commentary on Matthew's Gospel had brought on a relapse: "What was advantageous to the exercise of my tongue [he was, as usual, dictating his work] injured the health of my body."

We have also a letter written to a priest named Rufinus — not Jerome's boyhood friend — in which Jerome discusses the judgment of Solomon. In the concluding paragraph of this letter Jerome asks to be pardoned if his words do not flow in their usual course, for a man who dictates rapidly says whatever comes into his head, and cannot stop to erase or correct.

In 398 a wealthy Spaniard sent six copyists to Bethlehem, as there was a scarcity of Latin scribes in Palestine. They were to make copies of all of Jerome's writings. The Spaniard, whose name was Lucinus, and his wife, Theodora, both dedicated themselves to celibacy and were planning a tour of Palestine. On this occasion Jerome was very cordial in inviting them to visit him in Bethlehem. A later letter of sympathy to the widow indicates that Lucinus had died before he could undertake the pilgrimage. In this letter to Theodora, Jerome shows his constant loyalty to orthodoxy by a reference to Basilides, the Gnostic, and the heresy known as Priscillianism, which was then raging in Spain. This heresy asserted, among other things, that the soul shared in the divine substance, and denied the resurrection of the body.

Jerome also wrote a letter to a blind man in Spain, not personally known to him, a certain Abigaus, to whom he commended the widowed Theodora, expressing the hope that she will persist in her plan of visiting the Holy Land.

Still another letter is addressed to Salvina, the daughter of King Gildo of Mauretania. In the opening paragraph Jerome expresses the hope that this will not seem like an attempt to ingratiate himself with the royal court, and seek friendship with those in high places. Salvina's husband Nebridius had died not long after their marriage. As she had decided to remain a widow, Jerome wrote to strengthen her in her resolve.

It is interesting to note that various old friends in Rome, or elsewhere in Italy asked Jerome from time to time to translate certain Old Testament books. Desiderius had asked for the Pentateuch in Latin. Chromatius wished him to undertake Paralipomenon (Chronicles). He translated Esdras (Ezra) for Domnion and Rogation; and at the request of Paula and Eustochium he made a Latin version of the book of Esther.

It has already been pointed out that during the last twenty years of his life Jerome was more interested in the Old Testament than in the New. But Eusebius of Cremona prevailed upon him to write a commentary on St. Matthew's Gospel — the last New Testament book he studied.

Eusebius had spent some time at Bethlehem, and planned to return to Rome by Easter in 398. It was only in Lent of that year that Jerome's long continued fever began to abate. In spite of his illness and weakness, Jerome dictated the commentary on Matthew within the short space of two weeks.

As might have been expected, Jerome's writings record his general interests at the time of composition. So this work is filled with arguments against Origen, who had also written a commentary on Matthew. But he refuses to accept Origen's views on transmigration and the pre-existence of the soul, and various other heterodox beliefs.

Jerome's commentary contains citations from the Hebrew gospel perhaps not contained in Origen's work. While still in Rome, Jerome had believed this to be identical with Matthew's Gospel in Greek. Now that he had translated it from the Aramaic he had found that there are differences. In his commentary Jerome carefully explains a number of Hebrew words: e.g., raca, mammon, Beelzebub, and gehenna.

Eusebius had asked for a historical commentary, but Jerome added allegorical meanings as well. One point of interest is the fact that Jerome interprets the phrase "our daily bread" in the Lord's prayer as referring to Christ, the bread of life.

The fifteen years from 385 to 400, when Jerome practically completed his great Latin translation of the Bible, were the most productive years of his life.

At this same period Jerome's admiration for Origen, whose scholarship and literary achievement he was peculiarly qualified to appreciate, began to undergo a change. As Jerome became increasingly hostile to mistaken views in the field of theology, he became more critical of heretical doctrine. And as he became more and more the great champion of orthodoxy, he inevitably changed his opinion of those branded by the orthodox Church as heretics. Jerome's later years were filled with controversy.

CHAPTER VI - JEROME AND ORIGEN

As THE fourth century of the Christian era drew toward its close, it was becoming increasingly evident that the Church must take a definite stand on the question of Origen's theology. Jerome had praised him as a religious teacher second only to the Apostles. And, as a matter of fact, Origen was the founder of a new system of theology, and the acknowledged master of the allegorical interpretation of Sacred Scripture. It has been said that both the Arian heresy and Nicaean orthodoxy found their source in his speculations.

Bishop Epiphanius of Salamis, an old friend of Jerome as well as of Paula and Eustochium, and a strong supporter of the traditional theology, started the battle by writing, in 376, a book dealing with the great heretics of all time.

There is extant among Jerome's letters his translation of an epistle of Epiphanius of Cyprus addressed to Bishop John of Jerusalem. The original had been written in Greek. In it Epiphanius says: "You ought not to praise [Origen] *the father of Arius and the root and cause of the other heresies.*" And he continues: "In defense of heresy, you arouse ill-feeling against me, destroying the affection that I cherished for you. You have made me repent of having held communication with you, who so zealously defend the errors and dogmas of Origen."

Then in 393 a violent anti-Origenist named Aterbius ar-

The author at St. Jerome's burial place.

The grave of Paula and her daughter Eustochium, opposite
that of Jerome.

Albrecht Dürer's *Jerome in the Cell.*

rived in Jerusalem. He was perhaps an emissary of Epiphanius. At all events, he demanded from both Jerome and his old friend Rufinus a definite statement regarding their attitude toward Origen. During the interval from 386 to 393, Jerome and Rufinus, in spite of their boyhood friendship and the fact that they were both now living in the Holy Land, had apparently ignored each other. We find no mention in Jerome's writings during those years of either Rufinus or his patroness Melania. Yet, since 378 Rufinus had been living in Jerusalem, in the monastery that Melania had built on the Mount of Olives.

It will be recalled that both Rufinus and Jerome had studied under Didymus in Egypt: Rufinus for eight years; Jerome for a much shorter time. Two of Rufinus' closest friends there during this period of discipleship had been advanced to important bishoprics: Theophilus in Alexandria, in 385; John in Jerusalem the following year. Both of these men, like Rufinus himself, were stanch supporters of Origen, whom they had accepted on the authority of Didymus.

Upon the arrival of Aterbius in Palestine, Jerome (in response to his challenge) openly condemned the teaching of Origen, his once revered teacher and model. But it is important to note that Jerome had studied only the exegetical writings of Origen, admiring his skill in allegory. Jerome, accordingly, had never been knowingly heterodox or heretical. As soon as Origen's heresies were pointed out to him, Jerome unhesitatingly condemned them.

Rufinus refused to see Aterbius and was therefore accused of heresy. And his old friend Bishop John of Jerusalem naturally supported Rufinus.

The change in Jerome's attitude is shown by comparing his present position with a work written perhaps at his friend's request, before 392. This brief and rather superficial commentary on the Psalms was based not on his own translation of the Psalter from the Hebrew, but on the older Latin version still in general use at the time. The important point of interest in regard to this commentary is that it is largely based upon the work of Origen, and that Jerome praises Origen unreservedly in his prologue.

In 397, after a reconciliation with Jerome, which they sealed by receiving Communion together in the Church of the Resurrection in Jerusalem, Rufinus undertook a journey to Rome. To the end, however, Rufinus continued to be a follower of Origen. He seems now to cherish the desire which once animated Jerome: to become the mediator to the West of the great theological works of Origen. Jerome, meanwhile, was trying to free the Church — in both the East and the West — from Origen's heretical views.

In a letter to Vigilantius written in 398, Jerome says that he read Origen's work just as he read Apollinaris and others whose books on certain subjects the Church does not accept: "not because I declare that everything contained in their volumes is to be condemned, but because I admit that certain views are to be rejected." He is following the admonition of Paul: "Test all things; hold fast that which is good." And a little later he says: "Origen is a heretic. How does that concern me, since I do not deny that he is a heretic in many teachings." Then he proceeds to list Origen's chief heresies: "He was wrong about the resurrection of the body; he was wrong about the status of souls, about the repentance of the devil and — what is more serious than these — he stated that the Son and the Holy Spirit are seraphim" (cf. Letter 61:2, 1).

Vigilantius had been sent to Bethlehem by Paulinus of Nola to see Jerome. They were not congenial. Later each accused the other of Origenism.

When Rufinus reached Rome in 398, he found great unrest and uncertainty with regard to what Christians should believe. At the request of a friend named Macarius, he translated Origen's work on "First Principles" — perhaps his most controversial book. As translator, Rufinus claimed the right to omit various passages which he said had doubtless been inserted by some heretic. He took the point of view that where contradictions occur in Origen's works, the text must have been altered. There have been interpolations, he says.

The effect of this new translation by Rufinus was just the reverse of what he had intended. He had hoped to create propaganda for Origen in the West. Instead Origen was branded as a heretic.

Yet many were in doubt, particularly with regard to the dependability of the translation by Rufinus. And so his friends in Rome, Pammachius and Oceanus, now wrote to Jerome and asked him to translate the same book that they might compare it with the version that had aroused so much uncertainty and debate. They asked for a literal translation, and also for a clear statement of Jerome's own position with regard to Origen. Although he had been seeking some middle way, Jerome now found himself forced to take a definite stand against Origenism. He realized the vital importance of this request and therefore put aside all other work for the time being. He left incomplete his monograph against Bishop John of Jerusalem, and postponed his commentary on the prophet Daniel.

First he wrote a long and detailed letter to Pammachius and Oceanus, in which he makes clear his own position. He declares that he has always admired Origen's exegetical methods, but not his theology: "I praised quite simply his simple interpretation and method of teaching. . . . I praised the interpreter, not the dogmatist; his genius, not the apostle." He then calls attention to what he has said in his commentaries on Ecclesiastes and on Paul's Epistle to the Ephesians that is critical of Origen's theological views. He again lists the doctrines of Origen that he does not accept and that must be repudiated. Although abjuring his heretical views, Jerome insists that Origen was a great scholar and a great man.

He did not accept the theory of Rufinus that the heretical passages in "First Principles" were interpolated. In a letter no longer extant Rufinus had told Jerome that he was leaving Rome for Aquileia, where he hoped to see his spiritual father, Bishop Chromatius. Jerome, in a reply that reached Rome after Rufinus' departure, and was not forwarded to him, says that his brother Paulinian, who left Palestine for Rome in 398 — a year later than Rufinus — is now on his way to Stridon. They will probably see each other in Aquileia.

When Pammachius received Jerome's literal and accurate translation of Origen's "First Principles," he looked upon Rufinus as a heretic. However, Pope Siricius, who seems never to have been very favorably inclined toward Jerome, assured Rufinus that he was in full communion with the Roman Church. Jerome's conclusion is that the Origenists have succeeded in winning over Pope Siricius!

Siricius died in November of 399, and Pope Anastasius, who succeeded him, was definitely opposed to Origen.

ORIGENISM IN THE NEAR EAST

To return to the Near East, in Palestine the attack on John of Jerusalem and Rufinus by Bishop Epiphanius of Salamis (whom Jerome had supported) had been inconclusive. At first Bishop Theophilus of Alexandria had intervened as mediator. But in 399 he suddenly became the champion of orthodoxy, endeavoring to have Origen condemned as a heretic and his followers annihilated. Possibly he was trying to make himself supreme over Antioch and Constantinople. He had protested — vainly — against the election of Chrysostom as Bishop of Constantinople in 398. He sacrificed his friendship for the priest Isidore for theological reasons, and forced Bishop John of Jerusalem to join him. Late in the year 399 Theophilus called a synod of bishops to meet near Alexandria in order to condemn the heresy. Thence he proceeded to Nitria — earlier visited by Jerome, Paula, and Eustochium — where he read and condemned passages from Origen's writings in the presence of monks from all Egypt.

Many of the monks, in their ignorant enthusiasm for Origen, mutilated themselves to prove that they were good Christians, cutting off their ears or the tips of their tongues, and declaring that they would rather be burned alive than see Origen's writings condemned. As though they were proclaiming (says Theophilus): "We have placed our hope in lies, and by falsehood we are protected!" This appropriate verse he found in Isaias (Isaiah).

They then marched on Alexandria, joined by a crowd of slaves and beggars, in an attempt to force the Bishop to retract his decree of excommunication. Many of the rabble, we are told, were armed and ready for any crime for the sake of their gullets and bellies! When they reached their goal, they hid their clubs and other weapons in palm branches: "under the emblems of peace they concealed hearts that were prepared for slaughter."

The priest Isidore, with whom Theophilus had quarreled, now became the leader of the Origenists in Egypt. They even sought to win the help of pagans who were aroused by the destruction of their Serapeum.

Theophilus had sent Priscus and Eubulus as couriers to Bethlehem to inform Jerome of the condemnation of the supporters of Origen at the Council of Alexandria. Now he organized a crusade against Origenism in Palestine, and persuaded both Jerome and Epiphanius to assist him. In a letter to Theophilus, Jerome reports how the "vipers" were hunted from their lairs. "You have shown," he says, "that up to now silence meant pardon — not consent."

In this same letter Jerome defends his former opponent, John of Jerusalem; so it is evident that the two had become reconciled in the meantime.

Bishop Theophilus notified the bishops of Palestine, assembled in Jerusalem to attend a festival, that the Origenists had been officially condemned. In a letter signed by Bishop

John of Jerusalem and Eulogius of Caesarea, they all thus concurred in this action.

Not content with this success in Egypt and Palestine, Bishop Theophilus had also written to Epiphanius, asking him to call a synod of the Cyprian bishops to condemn Origen. Furthermore, knowing that several of the followers of Origen had taken refuge at Constantinople, he asked that copies of the proceedings against Origen should be sent to that city. Finally, he wrote to Pope Anastasius at Rome, asking him to condemn Origen. Jerome seems to have co-operated willingly; in fact, he told Theophilus that he had already written to Anastasius independently.

From Vincentius, who had journeyed to Rome before 397 and had recently returned to Palestine, Jerome learned that Origen had been condemned there also, and that Italy was free from all heresy.

Epiphanius and Jerome were triumphant. Adapting a verse in the book of Exodus, Epiphanius writes exultantly: "Write this for a memorial, that I will utterly destroy the heresy of Origen from the face of the earth."

In his letter written as a memorial to his old friend Marcella at Rome, Jerome gives her the chief credit for having secured this condemnation in the see of Peter. However, in all probability, Pammachius and Oceanus had played their part also.

The influence exerted by Eusebius of Cremona, too, was significant. We know that he had secured the translation of "The First Principles" by Rufinus even before it was finished. During the controversy between Jerome and John of

Jerusalem, Eusebius had been staying in Bethlehem. It was for him that Jerome had translated into Latin the letter of Epiphanius addressed to John.

Pope Anastasius declared that he was induced by the letter of "the holy and honorable Theophilus, our brother and fellow-bishop" to condemn Origenism. He quotes Paul's admonition to the Galatians: "But even if we or an angel from heaven should preach a gospel to you other than that which we have preached to you, let him be anathema!" So he condemns whatever Origen has written that is contrary to the orthodox faith. He now sends Eusebius of Cremona with excerpts from the heretical "First Principles" of Origen to Bishop Simplicianus of Milan, in order to induce him to take similar action. When Simplicianus died, Pope Anastasius likewise wrote to his successor, Venerius, a letter demanding that he accede to the unanimous decision of the Church.

It is evident from all this how completely Rufinus had failed in his endeavor to win Rome for Origenism. As already mentioned, he had withdrawn to Aquileia to see his old friend Bishop Chromatius. Rufinus felt that Jerome was responsible for his lack of success.

Apronianus forwarded to Rufinus at Aquileia the letter which Jerome had written to Pammachius and Oceanus in answer to their request that he should clear himself from the suspicion of complicity with Rufinus in the heresy of Origenism. Thereupon, in order to purge himself from the charge of heresy, Rufinus sent a defense to Anastasius. The pope summoned him to appear before a synod in Rome. He did not go. He could not be brought to trial, however,

as he had proclaimed his acceptance of the orthodox theological beliefs, disclaiming all responsibility for the views
of Origen as expressed in the "First Principles." He declared
that he had merely translated it at the request of friends.
His old associate John of Jerusalem, now at least nominally
orthodox, also wrote to the pope on behalf of Rufinus. In
spite of all this Rufinus was mistrusted.

Venerius of Milan had been influenced by Anastasius'
letter and condemned Origenism. Rufinus' friend Bishop
Chromatius of Aquileia followed his example. Finally, the
emperors Arcadius and Honorius forbade the reading of
Origen's books. So Church and State alike declared his views
heretical.

CHAPTER VII - JEROME AND RUFINUS: IS JEROME A HYPOCRITE?

WHAT effect had all this on the friendship between Jerome and Rufinus — originating in boyhood intimacy, but apparently allowed to lapse in recent years in spite of propinquity as well as similarity of tastes? Just as Jerome's early work dealing with Malchus the Captive Monk (A.D. 390) is of great importance for the light it sheds on the five years he spent in the desert of Chalcis, so the two books of "The Defense of Rufinus" (400), directed against Jerome, and the three books written (in 402) by the latter in reply are invaluable as evidence revealing the personalities and characters of these two distinguished clerics during the closing years of their lives.

Unfortunately, the personal letter sent by Jerome to Rufinus to explain the position in which he found himself when he made his literal and unabridged translation of Origen's "First Principles" was never received by Rufinus.

The "Defense" was, as we shall see, more of an attack on Jerome. Jerome replied in two books of invective before he had the authorized text of his friend's book before him. He published a third book a little later.

Aside from a number of minor criticisms, Rufinus assails Jerome on three principal charges: hypocrisy, perjury, and blasphemy. We shall consider these in order, and somewhat in detail.

To prove that he himself is not a heretic, Rufinus begins by referring to his baptism at Aquileia and his sponsors, Chromatius, Jovinus, and Eusebius — now all bishops — and declares his full acceptance of the orthodox Catholic faith.

He explains the circumstances that led to his undertaking to translate into Latin Origen's "First Principles": it was in response to a request made by a certain Macarius, a man renowned for learning and of blameless life. Furthermore, Rufinus says that in the preface he first set forth his own good faith.

We begin to mistrust the writer's good faith when he mentions the fact that Jerome has previously translated many of Origen's books. For by saying — as he does — "I am following him to the best of my ability," he is involving Jerome in his own condemnation while pretending to praise him. "I ask you," Rufinus inquires, "what crime I have committed if I have done what you did?"

How inconsistent Jerome is in now calling Origen a heretic (says Rufinus), whereas for the past thirty years he has referred to him in his prefaces as "a teacher of the church second only to the apostles." He declares that Jerome based his commentary on Ephesians upon Origen's earlier work, but without acknowledging his indebtedness. "You don't deny that you are his pupil," he says, "and you admit betraying him." Thus there emerges the first of the three accusations which Rufinus makes against Jerome: that of hypocrisy. He quotes a statement made by Jerome: "the city of Rome agrees on his condemnation . . . because they could not endure the glory of his eloquence and of his knowledge." And now Jerome has changed his tune and denounces Origen as a heretic!

Rufinus declares with truth that while trying to stamp out heretical doctrines men assail even their friends — apparently unaware of how well his own conduct proves that those accused of heresy are equally unscrupulous in defending themselves. Indeed, his very next statement is a threat to expose the contents of a confidential letter which will undoubtedly bring disaster upon Jerome but "which I do not wish to divulge prematurely." This threat sounds like a species of blackmail.

Rufinus depicts Jerome as wholly without truth, faith, or religion, and lacking all comprehension of the meaning of justice. His tongue is ever engaged in assailing his brethren (says Rufinus), his heart is filled with strife, his mind with envy and malice.

In a closing paragraph written perhaps as a postscript after the verdict has been rendered in the heresy trial at Rome, Rufinus declares that the condemnation of Origen carries with it the condemnation of Jerome. For whatever is condemned in the Greek is naturally condemned also in Latin — and the author should, of course, be condemned with the book. Thus he confuses the issue by identifying the translator with the author. Thus the "Defense" has resolved itself into an indictment of his "friend and good brother from the East."

Let us consider next Jerome's reply to this charge of hypocrisy. It is true, he says, that he also has translated Origen's "First Principles." It was a letter from Pammachius that induced him to make a correct and unabridged translation of this book. His purpose in undertaking the task was twofold: to show that Origen was a heretic; and to discredit an unreliable translation, namely that by Rufinus.

As Rufinus truly states, Jerome has translated many books by Origen in the course of the years: a total of seventy, in fact. Nevertheless, he says: "I never caused anyone to stumble" by setting forth heretical doctrines. Rufinus, on the other hand, emerged from obscurity for his rashness in translating a single volume.

In a moving passage, Jerome speaks to his boyhood friend with the utmost kindness: "I beg you to hear me with patience," he says. "It's your old friend who is expostulating with you. An accusation against a brother displeases me even when it is true."

Jerome explains why he does not always mention his sources. It is his custom to state first his own view, then the opposing view of Origen, finally the simple explanation of Apollinaris. He doesn't like to criticize by name those to whom he is in part indebted. "Unless you find the same statement in the Greek," he says, "consider whatever is said to be my own." This is a clear-cut and convincing reply to the charge of plagiarism, for Jerome lists his sources, once for all, in the prefaces to his commentaries.

If Rufinus had made a reliable translation, says Jerome, it would have been unnecessary for Jerome to replace his false interpretation by a true one. After all, what right had Rufinus to expurgate passages of Origen's book?

In his preface, Rufinus declares that he has eliminated all heretical matter. That, of course, makes him personally responsible for any heresies to be found in his translation. Jerome, on the other hand, in making a Latin translation of the same work, pointed out what doctrines the reader should avoid.

As a matter of fact (Jerome points out) heretics may be orthodox in some of their beliefs. Take, for example, their old teacher Didymus. He was orthodox in his view of the Trinity, and it was this book that Jerome translated into Latin, in response to a request made by Pope Damasus. Jerome admired Origen's knowledge of Scripture — but without accepting his heretical views.

Finally in his third book — his "Final Response" to Rufinus — Jerome asks: "Don't you see that your lies don't hang together? You say of your book that the work was incomplete, that it was stolen, that no one — or only a few — had copies. Take the title of your work," continues Jerome. "Aren't you ashamed to call your accusation *A Defense?*"

In a rather pathetic paragraph, Jerome again calls Jesus to witness that it is against his will that he has descended to recriminations. "How can it edify our hearers to have two old men fiercely assail each other on account of heretics? Why not clasp hands? We made mistakes as young men; let us amend our ways now that we are old. You forgive me because in my youth I praised Origen's erudition and zeal for Scripture, before I fully understood his heresy, and I'll pardon you for writing a defense of his books now that your head is gray."

How vividly the kindly spirit of the aged Jerome stands

out here in contrast with the bitter caviling of his boyhood friend Rufinus!

Jerome cherishes the friendship of Rufinus, but says: "If I cannot be your friend without being the friend of heretics, I shall endure your enmity with more ease than their friendship."

It is interesting to note, in this connection, that whenever Jerome speaks sharply of a person, it is because of their differing views on theological questions. Jerome will not compromise on matters of faith, regardless of personal ties.

"Do you want me to keep still?" asks Jerome. "Then don't accuse me. Put down your sword and I'll cast aside my shield. But in one point I can't agree with you: that I should spare heretics so that you may prove I'm not a Catholic."

After all, their whole quarrel is based on difference in religious belief. To that there can be but one answer. Jerome can give no quarter to heresy.

JEROME AND RUFINUS: IS JEROME GUILTY OF PERJURY AND BLASPHEMY?

While Rufinus' first accusation — that of being hypocritical and denying that he was as guilty of heresy as Rufinus — had at least some apparent basis, and may have been argued with sincerity, the second accusation — perjury — seems too absurd to be taken seriously.

Rufinus calls Jerome a perjurer because he broke the oath (which he took at the time of his famous dream) not to read the pagan classics. He states, with truth, that there is scarcely a page in Jerome's writings in which he does not quote from or refer to Cicero.

Rufinus further accuses Jerome of seeking the fame of being a great scholar: he boasts, in fact, of having read among others the works of Pythagoras "which, as learned men declare, do not even exist!" He criticizes the great biblical scholar for quoting from Horace and Cicero and Vergil instead of from Sacred Scripture in writing to girls and women for their edification. In some of his works, says Rufinus, Jerome inserts whole chapters from Cicero. He even indulges in an ill-timed jest. Referring to the work which Jerome entitled "On the best kind of Interpretation," aside from its title, he says, there's nothing "best" about it. It is absolutely the worst.

There is an interesting personal reference when Rufinus says: "before his conversion he was, like me, entirely ignorant of the Greek literature and language." And then he remarks, rather brutally: "As I see it, brother, you got off to a wrong start, since Porphyry introduced you to it." For Porphyry tried by his writings utterly to destroy the Christian religion.

Rufinus makes an interesting accusation when he claims that Jerome employed scribes to work in the monastery founded by Melania and Rufinus on the Mount of Olives, copying pagan (that is, classical) manuscripts — and paid them more than the regular rates for the copying of the Bible! "I know all about it," Rufinus declares. Worst of all, Jerome actually teaches the classics to his pupils at Bethlehem instead of putting the fear of God into them!

In answering the charge of perjury, Jerome remarks that

Rufinus is trying to exact from a sleeper conduct he himself never demonstrated when awake! As to the quibble about claiming to have read nonexistent books, Jerome never claimed that he had actually read a book *by* Pythagoras. He had read *about* his philosophy in Cicero. "I said I had read his *teachings*," says Jerome, "not his books."

As to the dream: "I said I would not read secular literature in future," he explains. "I did not make a vow to abolish past memories." And he adds: "Who of us does not remember his childhood?"

He pays his friend a compliment when he says: "Are you surprised at my not forgetting my Latin literature when you learned Greek without a teacher?"

But the real answer to the accusation of perjury comes at the close of his discussion. "That's what I'd say," he concludes, "if I'd promised any such thing while I was awake!" The vow was part of the dream itself.

So Jerome quite reasonably remarks that, after all, we must not put too much faith in dreams. "How often I've seen myself dead and buried — in dreams," he says.

Finally he challenges his friend, saying: "You expect me to keep a promise made in a dream. Have you kept all the promises you made when you were baptized? Has either of us lived up to all the demands implied by the word 'monk'?"

Surely no one can feel that the charge of perjury made by Rufinus is more than a rather malicious attack upon Jerome's known love for the great classical writers of antiquity.

That brings us, finally, to the most unreasonable attack

of all — his criticism of Jerome's greatest work, the Vulgate translation of the Bible. Rufinus seems convinced that the Greek version of the Old Testament, the Septuagint, miraculously given to the Greek-speaking world before Christ's coming, is authoritative and final. He mistrusts Hebrew texts and Hebrew teachers. So he remarks with a sneer: "unless, of course, under a new dispensation, truth is divulged to the Church by certain Jews."

And so Rufinus belittles Jerome's study of Hebrew under Baranina. "Pardon me," he says, "but I'd rather seem ignorant and unlearned than be numbered with the pupils of Barabbas!" Amusing, perhaps, but rather cheap wit. Especially as he goes on to remark pompously: "When Christ and Barabbas were set before us, I — the unlearned — chose Christ!"

Very unfairly, as it appears to us today, Rufinus inquires why Jerome had thought it necessary to make a new translation of the Bible — "new at this late date, and actually borrowed from the Jews!" How are we to regard it: as divine or human? He stands aghast at Jerome's temerity.

Rufinus unreasonably claims greater authority for the Septuagint than for a version "made by one man — though with the inspiration of Barabbas!" Apparently Rufinus accepts the legend that the seventy-two men worked in separate cells and by divine aid produced identical translations of the Hebrew original.

Recall, to summarize Rufinus' argument, that the Apostle Peter — pope for twenty-four years — never put forth a new Bible. Did he deceive the Church of Christ, permitting

Christians to have a false account of the gospel story, although he knew that the truth was current among the Jews? Suppose — for the sake of argument — that Peter was incapable of doing what Jerome has just done — what of Paul? He was not an unlearned man, was he? Can it be that the Church has been wrong for four hundred years? Moreover, how can pagans believe the Bible a divine book now that it has been changed — amended — by a mere man! And so Rufinus rejects Jerome's Vulgate saying: "I want no wisdom which Peter and Paul did not teach. I want no truth that lacks the approval of the apostles." We are reminded of the medieval astronomer who refused to look through a telescope for fear he would see something that Aristotle had not seen!

But Rufinus goes still further. He declares that in his letter to Eustochium on the celibate life (Ep. 22) Jerome is impious — actually blasphemous. He wonders whether it has escaped his notice that in calling the girl to whom he is writing "the bride of Christ" he is by implication giving her mother in the flesh the title of "mother-in-law of God!"

Now let us see how Jerome answered this ultimate accusation. Quite properly he expresses his resentment and indignation at a trick played upon him. A forged letter, purporting to be a repentant confession of his guilt in translating into Latin, as the Bible, Hebrew books in which there was no truth, has been circulated in Africa. "I was thunderstruck to hear of it," he says. And he concludes: "a man who would have the audacity to do a thing like that would dare do anything." In a later passage (in his third book) Jerome declares his conviction that it was Rufinus who forged the letter and circulated it among the churches of Africa.

In answer to the accusation that he had belittled the Septuagint version of the Old Testament, Jerome points out the absurdity of such a statement. "Why," he says, "all my biblical commentaries are based on the Septuagint as well as on my own new text!"

Jerome makes evident the reason for a re-translation of Scripture by pointing out phrases and whole sentences found in the Hebrew but not in the Greek — like "I called my son out of Egypt" (Osee [Hosea] 11:1).

Surely, says Jerome, we cannot accept the myth about the inspiration of the Septuagint — the separate cells in which as many translators produced an identical Greek version! And, as a matter of fact, Josephus tells us that they assembled in a single basilica. They were scholars, not prophets.

Jerome's translation of the Old Testament differs from theirs in at least one important particular. He is in a position to speak of Christ's passion and resurrection from the viewpoint of history. These things have actually come to pass since the Septuagint version was written. So Jerome says, very impressively: "I do not reject, I do not criticize the Seventy. But I confidently prefer the apostles to them all. It is through their words that Christ speaks to me."

Jerome points out that when Jesus quoted from the Old Testament, it was from Hebrew Scripture. "But I have at least a slight knowledge of Hebrew," he says, "and am not entirely without facility in the Latin language [a magnificent example of understatement] so I can form a better judgment about other versions of the Bible and can express in our own tongue what I myself understand."

Why should he, a Christian and born of Christian parents, who bears on his brow the sign of the cross, whose purpose has ever been to restore what was omitted, to correct what has been distorted, and to reveal in clear and accurate language the sacraments of the Church — why should he be rebuked by opinionated or spiteful readers? To be sure, the envious despise what they themselves cannot do.

Jerome makes a very modest request for his new translation of Scripture: "Let them at least deign to keep it as one version — after those that have preceded it." And, above all, "Let them read it before they despise it." Still, Jerome remarks, no one who doesn't care to is obliged to read the book.

Surely the charge of blasphemy brought by Rufinus against Jerome is not substantiated. And, more important still, Jerome the aged stands revealed by his words as a true and lovable character, somewhat crabbed, perhaps, but free from guile and from misrepresentation.

TROUBLES AND SORROWS MULTIPLY

It was apparently in 401 that Jerome wrote his counterattack on Rufinus, immediately after his brother Paulinian returned to Bethlehem. Like so many of Jerome's writings, this letter seems to have been composed with extreme rapidity. When finished, it was taken to Rufinus (who was at Aquileia) by a messenger who stayed for only two days. The letter he brought back from Rufinus in reply has un-

fortunately not come down to us. With this reply he brought
to Jerome the two books of the original invective as well;
these Jerome had not yet seen, although he was aware of
their contents. The third book of Jerome's "Apology" was
written after he had these authentic writings in his possession. The name is, of course, a misnomer: it was more of an
attack than a defense.

We learn from this "final reply" by Jerome to Rufinus
that the latter regarded the letter from Pope Anastasius to
Bishop John (accusing Rufinus, but absolving Jerome) as
a forgery written by Jerome himself. He also refused to
acknowledge as authentic the letter that Jerome had sent
to him at the outbreak of the dispute.

We have only Jerome's account of this last letter of his
boyhood friend, but it shows Rufinus at his worst. Bishop
Chromatius, who was their mutual friend, sought to end
their disgraceful quarrel. Jerome told Chromatius that
silence on his part might be interpreted by Rufinus as evidence of a guilty conscience. Nevertheless, after a passage
in his last book to Rufinus which is marked by bitter scorn,
Jerome suddenly turned to a moving and evidently heartfelt
plea for reconciliation. To this Rufinus did not respond.

We know that Rufinus spent the rest of his life in translating Origen's writings — never so much as mentioning his
old friend Jerome. Between the years 406 and 408, when
the Goths were threatening Aquileia, Rufinus made his way
to Pinetum, the ancient pine forest that Jordanes, the Gothic
historian, mentions as one of the three parts of Ravenna.
The forest is still a notable landmark in that city. Here he
met, once more, his old friend Melania, her daughter Albina

and her grandchildren. In 409, the year before the sack of Rome by Alaric, Rufinus fled to Sicily. He died a year later at Messina. From his home there he was able to see Rhegium being burned by the barbarians.

It is sad to note that even after his friend's death Jerome continued to attack "the Scorpion," as he now called Rufinus. In the preface to his commentary on Ezechiel (Ezekiel) Jerome says: "The Scorpion lies underground between Enceladus and Porphyrion. The hydra of many heads has at last ceased to hiss at me." And in a letter to the monk Rusticus, written shortly before Rufinus' death, Jerome says: "The Grunter" — another epithet which he applied to Rufinus — "used to proceed to speak at a turtle's pace and scarcely got a few words out at fixed intervals. You might have supposed he had the hiccups, not that he was making a speech!" In another letter Jerome refers obscurely to Melania as "the lady whose name bears witness to the darkness of perfidy." Jerome was a good hater once he was convinced that a person was a heretic.

In the West, interest in the Origenist heresy largely died out upon the death of Pope Anastasius in 401. In the East, however, persecution of heretics continued. Perhaps Theophilus of Alexandria was using this means of overthrowing his rival John Chrysostom, of Constantinople. When Theophilus (who wrote in Greek) treated of the Origenist heresy in his Easter letters of 401, 402, and 404, Jerome translated these into Latin.

In his letter to Theophilus, in the spring of 404, we learn from the opening paragraph that Jerome had been overwhelmed by grief at the death of his dear friend Paula.

"I could scarcely translate your book into Latin," he says. "I was prostrated by the falling asleep of the holy and venerable Paula. And apart from the translation of this book I have written no other religious work up to the present."

Paula died on January 26, 404, and was buried in a smaller cave just outside Jerome's cell at Bethlehem. Later, when Eustochium died, she was interred in the same grave with her mother; and in 420 Jerome's body was laid to rest just across from theirs.

Eustochium could scarcely be torn from her mother's corpse. "She kissed her eyes, put her face against Paula's, embraced her body, and said that she wished to be buried with her mother."

In Paula's last illness Eustochium had been constantly by her side, acting as a most devoted nurse. When asked whether she was in pain, Paula replied in Greek that she was at peace. And so she died, in her fifty-seventh year, surrounded by friends. Jerome felt her loss almost as keenly as her daughter did, and wrote a beautiful memorial letter, a eulogy, of some forty-five pages.

The only poetry Jerome composed occurs in this epistle. At the close he celebrates in hexameters her noble ancestry, mentioning Scipio, Paulus, the Gracchi and Agamemnon as her forebears. Then he says: "Do you fail to appreciate this narrow tomb in the sheer rock? It is the resting-place of Paula, who abides in the heavenly kingdom. Forsaking her brother, her kindred and Rome, her native city, her wealth and her offspring, she is buried in a cave at Bethlehem. Here was your crib, O Christ, and here the kings brought their prophetic gifts and gave them to One who was both God and man."

Paula's son, Toxotius, had married Laeta, the daughter of the pagan pontifex at Rome. After giving birth to several dead children, Laeta had vowed to dedicate her next daughter, if she lived, to God's service as a nun. This child was named Paula, after her grandmother. Laeta had asked Jerome's advice regarding her child's education, and in his reply he urged that the girl should be sent to Bethlehem to be reared by her grandmother and her aunt Eustochium.

It was not until after the elder Paula's death, however, that her namesake came to Bethlehem to be educated and trained by her aunt, in compliance with this advice. Even though she never saw her little granddaughter, it had brought great joy to Paula that her beloved son Toxotius had finally consented to consecrate his only daughter, Paula, to virginity.

In 406 Jerome completed his commentaries on the last five prophets in what is called by the Hebrews "The Book of the Twelve" (i.e., the Minor Prophets): Zacharias (Zachariah), Malachias (Malachi), Osee (Hosea), Joel, and Amos. He had planned to dedicate the last three commentaries to Paula. Since she was dead, Jerome dedicated them to her son-in-law Toxotius instead.

Like his earlier commentaries, these, too, are based on both the Hebrew text and the Septuagint. Jerome states that Jesus, the apostles, and the evangelists sometimes cite the Old Testament from the Hebrew rather than from the Septuagint.

In his preface to Osee Jerome admits that in these last commentaries he is essentially a compiler, and names the writers he has followed. For his valuable historical commentary he is indebted chiefly to the Jews.

Occasionally he refers to current events. So in his commentary on Joel there is a reference to a plague of grasshoppers recently experienced in Judaea. He laments the devastation by barbarian hordes of Illyria, Thrace, Macedonia, Pannonia, and the entire region from the Bosphorus to the Julian Alps.

There is an odd reference to Athens. Jerome states that he saw on the Acropolis a very heavy iron ball, near the statue of Athena, which athletes were supposed to be able to lift. Jerome tried to lift it, but reports that he was unable to do so. The modern visitor will find on the Acropolis neither the statue of Athena nor the heavy iron ball.

Jerome was now a man in his middle sixties. He suffered a severe illness after Paula's death. No longer able to write, he was forced to dictate.

CHAPTER VIII - JEROME AS A TEACHER

For firsthand information regarding Jerome as a teacher we need only read such a letter as the interesting epistle written in 403 to Laeta, Paula's daughter-in-law. She had married Toxotius, the son and namesake of Paula's husband, Julius Toxotius, who had died in or about 379, and "in whose veins ran the noble blood of Aeneas." Laeta's daughter Paula was born in 397 and in infancy consecrated by her parents to God's service as a nun.

Paula's grandfather, Albinus, was a pagan and a Roman pontiff in the service of the older religion. Nevertheless Jerome expresses hope for his conversion to Christianity. "Who would have believed," asks Jerome, "that the pontiff Albinus would stand by and rejoice while the baby's stammering tongue cried 'Alleluia,' and that the old man would fondle in his arms a virgin of Christ!" "But" (he adds) "I think even Jupiter himself might have believed in Christ if he had had such devout kindred!" And he points out that Christians are not born but made.

We find an interesting picture of the changes in the City brought about since Constantine's personal acceptance of Christianity. The gilded dome of the Capitol — where Jupiter, Juno, and Minerva had been worshiped — has a dingy look. The temples of the old gods are covered with soot and cobwebs. The people hurry past to visit the graves of the martyrs instead.

A kinsman of Laeta bearing the proud name of Gracchus had destroyed the cave of Mithras when he was prefect of the city of Rome. The military standards now bear the emblem of the cross.

In the provinces the same thing was happening. In 389 the temple of Serapis at Alexandria had been destroyed and a Christian Church erected on the site. The Syrian god Marnas was no longer reverenced. Crowds of monks were pouring in from India, Persia, and Ethiopia. Even the Huns were committing the Psalms to memory, and the Getae carried church tents with them on their military campaigns! "Perhaps they fight with us on equal terms," says Jerome, "because they believe in the same religion."

But we have digressed (he remarks). I was going to advise you how to bring up this little seven-year-old girl!

The educational methods advocated by Jerome are amazingly modern and practical. He suggests making a set of letters, the Roman alphabet, for the child, out of some smooth, hard wood, or of ivory. She is to learn their names while she plays with them, "making a game of study." It is not enough to be able to repeat the alphabet by rote and in order. Mix the letters up, and let the child recognize them by sight also.

When she begins to write, let her trace with the stylus the letters that have been impressed by another hand on a wax tablet.

Jerome advocates prizes as incentives to success in spelling and gifts for achievement. Like Aristotle, the tutor of

Alexander the Great, Jerome feels that rivalry in learning is essential, and that the pupil should have companions in study. Praise for achievement is a better stimulant than blame for slowness of comprehension.

Jerome stresses the importance of vocabulary in learning to read: the words are not to be taken at haphazard. For a child who is to dedicate her life to the Christian religion, it would be well to familiarize her with the names of the prophets, the apostles, and the patriarchs — starting with Adam!

Jerome quite properly stresses the importance of the teacher's character. "One of approved years, life and learning should be chosen."

"The first impression made upon a child's mind is hard to remove." Children should never be taught, by precept or example, anything they will later be obliged to unlearn.

Religious instruction should be begun at an early age, and the child should be told about her other grandmother, Paula, and the aunt in Bethlehem whom she is to join later. She may even help to win her pagan grandfather Albinus to the Christian faith. She is to leap into his arms, hang from his neck, and sing out "Alleluia" — whether it pleases him or not! Poor old pagan grandfather!

Jerome warns the mother against loading the child down with jewelry, dying her hair with henna (for often the fires of Gehenna follow that in due course!) or painting and powdering her face.

Little Paula is to commit selections from Scripture to memory every day — in the original Greek as well as in her native Latin tongue.

Having learned, perhaps from the tragic fate of Blesilla, Jerome declares his opposition to prolonged fasting — especially for the young. "I have learned by experience," he says, "that the donkey on the road seeks an inn when weary." (We may picture Jerome riding about Palestine on a donkey during the last thirty-five years of his life — and perhaps occasionally trying to divert the interest shown by his mount in inns!)

Jerome displays critical ability with regard to the Bible, declaring that if Paula ever wishes to read the apocryphal books, she must realize that they were not actually written by those to whom they are attributed and that "it requires great skill to seek for gold in the mud!" Of later Christian writers, he recommends Cyprian, Athanasius, and Hilary.

When the time comes, after her early education, she is to be sent to the Holy Land to join the nuns at Bethlehem, under the instruction of her grandmother Paula, and her aunt Eustochium. "Place this most precious jewel in Mary's chamber, and put her in the crib where Jesus cried as an infant."

Jerome asks that she be taught on her grandmother's knee the lessons which Eustochium learned there. He promises to be both the teacher and the foster father of little Paula. "I will carry her on my shoulders," he says, "and though an old man, will direct her stammering speech."

When Paula's granddaughter and namesake came to Bethlehem, she was trained by her aunt Eustochium, in compliance with the advice given in the letter.

As a teacher, Jerome was far in advance of his age. He advocated visual education, for he declares: "Much more is understood through being seen by the eyes than by being taken in through the ears." Many of his common-sense views are being heralded today as "modern" and "progressive." "O how wonderful is the teacher's gift," he says. And of ignorant humanity in general: "Without a teacher they cannot achieve what they long for."

Jerome's definition of a teacher is this: as an orator is "a good man, skilled in speaking," so also does that person destroy all his influence as a teacher whose words are belied by his conduct. Character — goodness — is the first essential. Next comes knowledge. "It is the mark of an unworthy instructor to teach what you are ignorant of yourself; and not even know this — that you do not know." On the contrary, he says to teachers: "Spend a long time in learning what you are to teach."

Jerome himself was a born teacher. The words he spoke of another are notably applicable to himself: "He found everywhere something to learn, so that, always becoming more proficient, he ever became a better man." His lifelong desire was for the sincere and the genuine. He never confused ignorance with godliness. He had a burning desire for learning and for teaching. His intellectual curiosity was insatiable. Moreover he could recognize in others that love of wisdom which he himself possessed. "O that I might teach what I have learned," he cries, "and hand on, as it were, the mysteries of the prophets! Then there would arise among us [those of the Christian faith] something that learned Greece did not possess." And in the teaching of religious truth he was forever emphasizing that "the letter kills, but the spirit gives life."

In his commentary on Ezechiel (Ezekiel), written during the closing years of his life, Jerome gives us a glimpse of the difficulties under which he wrote. He speaks of the hardships of the times. Rome has been taken and sacked, and the barbarians are beginning their centuries of wandering and of destroying a civilization they can neither comprehend nor replace.

He is now dictating the work because of failing eyesight, because he cannot read the Hebrew texts by lamplight. Yet he declares that his work comforts him amid the sufferings and the injustice of the times. Finally, he lists three reasons for the obscurities in his commentary: the enormity of the task, the teacher's own lack of skill, the indifference of the hearer.

Are not these the difficulties with which every teacher still has to contend?

JEROME AND AUGUSTINE

Though possessed of different gifts, Jerome and Augustine were now the two greatest theologians of the Western church. Augustine was some fifteen years younger than Jerome, and was destined to survive him by ten years. They never met.

We are able to perceive their differing personalities in their extant correspondence. We have twelve letters from Augustine to Jerome, and nine from Jerome to Augustine, over a period of thirty years.

So far as we can tell from the extant letters, Augustine wrote first, in 394. He was at Hippo Regius, but not yet Bishop. In the preceding year, 393, Augustine's young friend

Alypius, with whom he had been baptized, had undertaken a pilgrimage to the Holy Land. There he had become personally acquainted with Jerome, and upon his return to Africa he informed Augustine of Jerome's scholarly writings. Augustine's first letter, in which he expressed his veneration for his fellow priest, was to have been delivered to Jerome by Profuturus, who was planning a pilgrimage. However, being chosen bishop at home, he did not go to Palestine. Not long afterward Profuturus died, and Augustine's letter was not delivered.

In 397 Augustine tried again, and this time his letter had a still stranger fate. Paulus (who was to deliver it) changed his itinerary, going to Rome instead of to Jerusalem. Here (though without the writer's knowledge) Augustine's letter became known to the circle of Jerome's friends and enemies. Not until 402— five years later — did Jerome himself finally receive an unsigned copy of this epistle. As the content of Augustine's letter was critical in nature, Jerome began to suspect that these letters he had failed to receive were intended to be read by others, and to compromise his writings. When Augustine heard about this, he wrote again saying (in an extant letter): "Know that this is not so. I call our God to witness that I did not do this."

In his first letter Augustine had expressed on behalf of the entire church of Africa a hope that Jerome would translate Origen's writings into Latin. By 402, as we know, Jerome had broken away from Origenism.

A second wish expressed by Augustine in that letter was that Jerome should translate the Old Testament from Origen's hexaplar text instead of from the Hebrew. This

Jerome had done in the case of the Book of Job. Augustine seems to have had little comprehension of the importance of Jerome's scholarship and the value of his great work — a Latin Bible based upon the original texts. He found it hard to believe that anything in the Hebrew text had escaped the notice of the earlier translators.

A third topic dealt with by Augustine in his letter to Jerome was the interpretation of a passage in Galatians (2:11 ff.): the dispute between Peter and Paul. Jerome had explained it as being apparent rather than real. This Augustine found himself unable to accept. In Augustine's second letter (written in 397, but not received by Jerome until 402) he asked Jerome for the proper title of his book containing a list of Christian writers. He says he has a copy, and finds it entitled *Epitaphium*. This cannot be correct, since it includes names of writers who are still living. He also criticizes Jerome for including heretics in his catalog of Christian writers without comment upon their doctrines. Then he brings up once more the disputed passage in Galatians.

Augustine holds that what Paul actually criticized Peter for was the practice of requiring a pagan to become a Jew as a step toward Christianity. He goes so far as to request Jerome to change his interpretation and publish a retraction of his former view. This Jerome would not do. "The sound of your voice can scarcely reach me," says Jerome, "separated from you by so great distances of sea and land, and if perchance you write a letter, Italy and Rome will receive it before I do — though I am the person to whom it should be delivered." Evidently he is still annoyed because others had read Augustine's criticisms of him before he himself had.

Although the misunderstanding was straightened out and he finally understood the strange vicissitudes of this attempted correspondence, Jerome was burdened by the long illness of his beloved Paula. He rejects a suggestion that he should criticize Augustine's writings; any attempt on his part would be childish. Jerome regrets the impossibility of their meeting and discussing together the things in which they are both so deeply interested. "I have run my course," he says; and being weary, he wishes only to be left in peace.

Before Jerome's reply had reached him, Augustine wrote again, availing himself of the opportunity of sending a letter by Deacon Cyprian, who was starting for the Holy Land. He now explains in detail why his earlier epistle had been so delayed.

It is strange that the entire correspondence between these two great contemporaries was subject to such hazards and misunderstandings. Jerome's reply appears to indicate that he does not altogether trust Augustine. Still he does not wish to quarrel with him. In a rather pathetic closing paragraph he calls Augustine "my very dear friend, in years a son, in station a father." Yet he asks him to make sure in future that he may be the first to read letters that are addressed to him!

Augustine, in a friendly and disarming reply, reminds Jerome that ten years have elapsed since that first letter. "I beseech you by the compassion of Christ," he says, "that if I have offended you, you will forgive me."

Augustine deplores the fact that Jerome and Rufinus,

once such close friends, should now be bitter enemies. "What friend is not to be looked upon with dread as a possible future enemy, if this misunderstanding, which I lament, could arise between Jerome and Rufinus?" He closes by expressing the hope that their present enmity may once more be transformed into friendship. This letter reminds one of the attempt — successful in that case — made by Petrarch, centuries later, to reconcile his estranged friends "Socrates" and "Laelius."

This letter from Augustine was delivered by a personal friend named Praesidius. Jerome replied in a long and careful letter in which he discusses the various points raised by Augustine, defending his own points of view. Then, before there was time for an answer, Jerome availed himself of the return journey of a certain Firmus from Bethlehem to Africa to send another letter. He declares himself eager to put an end to their prolonged literary controversy. What he seeks is friendship — brotherhood, rather. Augustine answered the last three missives of Jerome in a single detailed letter of considerable length.

Although Augustine refused to allow Jerome's new translation of the Bible to be read in the churches of Africa, upholding the Septuagint because the people are used to it and because "this translation was approved even by the apostles," he nevertheless admits that although he is superior in ecclesiastical rank, he is inferior to Jerome in many respects — presumably in scholarship and perhaps also in dialectical skill.

How often it happens — as, for example, in the case of

Goethe and Heine — that great contemporaries fail to appreciate each other. Today we realize the equal greatness, but differing capacities, of these two Fathers of the Church. Augustine was primarily a philosopher and a theologian. Jerome was essentially a scholar.

CHAPTER IX · THE CONTROVERSY AGAINST VIGILANTIUS, 403-406

VIGILANTIUS was a Gallic priest whom Sulpicius Severus had recommended to Paulinus of Nola, and he in turn to Jerome. He stayed for a time in Bethlehem in 396. But upon his return to the West, Vigilantius had accused Jerome of Origenism. Then, in 404, a priest named Riparius, whom Jerome had befriended and who was a neighbor of Vigilantius at Calagurrae in Aquitaine, denounced him to Jerome as a dangerous heretic. He was specific in his accusation, declaring that Vigilantius had assailed the cult of the saints, the reverence paid to sacred relics, the practice of celibacy and monasticism itself.

From that time on Jerome looked upon Vigilantius as a second Jovinian, against whose teachings he had written an invective in 391-392. As a matter of fact, Vigilantius was perhaps even more radical in his views than his predecessors, Helvidius and Jovinian.

Jerome wrote to Riparius in defense of the cult of the martyrs. "We pay honor to the remains of the martyrs," he says, "that we may show reverence for Him whose own the martyrs are." And he calls attention to the fact that when Moses died he was buried by God Himself "in the valley of the land of Moab over against Phogor." "Are the relics of Peter and Paul unclean then?" he asks. Vigilantius had declared that such excesses as he found in Christianity had their origin in pagan beliefs and practices. That is why Jerome assailed him so vehemently. "Do we then," asks Jerome, "as often as we enter the basilicas of the apostles and prophets and all the martyrs, pay reverence to temples of idols? And are the wax candles kindled before Christian tombs evidences of idolatry?" In that case the body of our Lord and the white-clad angels in the tomb must have shared in pollution and defilement!

Jerome remarks of Vigilantius that his name apparently goes by contraries: he should have been called "Dormitan-tius" — that is, "Sleepy-head," not "Wide-awake"! He con-siders Vigilantius to be of the company of Julian the Apostate, and says to him: "Go to school and get an educa-tion, that when you have learned everything you may at least begin to keep quiet."

Though he defended the cult of the martyrs, Jerome made a careful distinction between divine worship and reverence for the saints. In the year 787, at the Second Council of Nicaea, this distinction gained official recognition.

It was not until 406 that Jerome received from Riparius and a priest named Desiderius the monograph written by Vigilantius. He sent back by the same messenger, a monk named Sissinius, his own invective, written (he tells us) in a single night. He sent also his commentaries on Zacharias (Zechariah) and Malachias (Malachi) for Bishop Exuperius of Toulouse.

Jerome was always ready to write treatises in defense of

virginity — hence his polemical works directed against Helvidius, Jovinian, and Vigilantius.

The attack by Vigilantius upon everything that Jerome held dear so aroused him that in his reply Jerome had recourse to insulting personalities. He ridicules his opponent as the son of an innkeeper. He attacks his literary style, and does not hesitate to employ disagreeable invectives. However, this treatise does contain serious criticism as well. In it, Jerome confesses his deep faith which causes him to tremble in the presence of the martyrs because of his sins. He claims that since they follow the Lamb of God, the saints — like their Lord — are omnipresent.

In his attack on the monastic ideal, Vigilantius had asked who would be left to serve God in the churches if all were to enter monasteries and practice celibacy. Apparently the higher clergy in Aquitaine agreed with Vigilantius on this point, for in 405 Pope Innocent was obliged to write to Bishop Exuperius of Toulouse to forbid the clergy to marry.

There was another aspect of the Gallic situation that vitally affected Jerome's work in Bethlehem: the cessation of financial support from Gaul. Alms donated there were now to be expended there, on the theory that "charity begins at home." And since Paula's death Jerome was in need of funds. As early as 397 he had sent his brother Paulinian to Stridon to sell the ruins of their home there — whatever remained after the ravages of the barbarians — together with the land, that he might not be mocked for having started something that he could not finish. Bethlehem was being overrun by refugees from all over the world. So the loss of the contributions hitherto received from Gaul was a serious matter.

In spite of Jerome's certainty that he is wholly in the right in his attack on Vigilantius, the modern reader is not so sure. We do not know the outcome of the struggle. From another source we learn that Vigilantius was later a priest at Barcelona in Spain, but whether he was dislodged by Jerome's invectives or by an incursion of the Vandals is not known.

All this time Jerome was engaged in his chief literary work — the exposition of Scripture. In about the year 408, Jerome finished his commentary on the prophet Daniel. It contains little allegory, and throughout Jerome disputes with Porphyry the historical accuracy of the book. Porphyry regarded it as a record of past events.

Because the Greek text of the Septuagint translation differs widely from the Hebrew, Jerome used as a basis for this commentary his own translation from the Hebrew. But he states that in his translation certain portions not found in the Hebrew (and hence marked by an obelus) have come down in "Chaldean" — that is to say, in Aramaic. Jerome's commentary on Daniel is shorter than his earlier commentaries on Old Testament prophets, since it explains only the obscure passages.

Though there are few contemporaneous references, Jerome considers Rome to be the last of the four kingdoms mentioned in Daniel. He refers to the barbarian invasions and to the use of barbarian leaders in the army by Rome. This was interpreted as a veiled reference to the young

Western Emperor, Honorius, and his guardian, the Vandal Stilicho. Because of this passage Jerome was denounced by Stilicho in Rome. When Stilicho was put to death by the Emperor in 408, Jerome looked upon the event as a judgment of God.

During the years 408–410, Jerome was occupied with his commentary on Isaias, the longest prophetical book of the Old Testament. Many years before, as a pupil of Gregory of Nazianzus in Constantinople, Jerome had written a brief tractate on the sixth chapter of Isaias. Later, in 397, he had written (at the request of Bishop Amabilis), a historical explanation of the ten visions of Isaias, contained in chapters 13–23. This he took over unchanged as the fifth book of his commentary. But in his sixth and seventh books he again explains these same chapters allegorically.

Jerome lists his sources in the preface to his first book. However, what makes his commentary unique is the fact that he also used Hebrew commentaries which he had received orally from his teachers. Nevertheless he often rejects the Hebrew for a Christian interpretation.

In the Isaias commentary Jerome makes frequent allusions to contemporaneous events. He sees God's judgment upon Rome in the invasions of the Huns.

It is perhaps worthy of note that Jerome attributes the entire book to a single author, indicating no division at chapter 40, where modern scholars hold that the second Isaias starts. He also attributed to Isaias chapters 36–39, in which the prophet is referred to in the third person. This passage is actually an excerpt from the Book of Kings.

Just as he was finishing his commentary on Isaias, Jerome

received the devastating news of the death of his friends Marcella and Pammachius amid the general destruction of Rome — sacked by Alaric the Goth in 410.

But Christ softened the hearts of the Goths, says Jerome in his memorial to his beloved friend Marcella, written two years later. They were prevailed upon to spare Marcella and Principia, who were conducted to the basilica of St. Paul for protection. For Alaric had ordered that all who took refuge in the churches were to be spared.

But the barbarian invasions were not confined to Italy.

BARBARIAN INVASIONS

As early as 405 or 406 Jerome reports an attack of Isaurian marauders who ravaged Phoenicia and Galilee, and whose further advance was feared by Judaea. Before long, news from the West told of the barbarian hordes that were crossing the Alps into Gaul. As many as ten or a dozen different tribes overran the entire country between the Alps and the Pyrenees, and between the Ocean and the Rhine. Spain, too, was living in fear.

Of course the Danube frontier of the Roman Empire had been penetrated long before this. The entire country between the Black Sea and the Julian Alps had already been alienated from the Roman Empire for thirty years. Rome had long paid "protection money" to the barbarians, and was now fighting for her life. "Except for a few old men," says Jerome, "all had been born in captivity and a state of siege. They did not long for liberty. They had never known it."

Jerome is shocked at the realization that Rome no longer

fights for glory, but only for survival. She does not even fight, but pays for the privilege of living with gold. He says that "a semi-barbarous traitor" — doubtless the reference is to Stilicho — has armed their foes by the expenditure of Roman money.

It was a time when one might behold on every hand the death of friends and of fellow citizens, and the destruction of country estates and entire cities.

But in 410 the greatest calamity of all occurred. Rome itself was sacked by Alaric the Goth. Eight hundred years had elapsed since such a disaster had previously befallen the city on the Tiber. Jerome could scarcely credit the tidings. "A dreadful rumor reached us from the West," he writes. "We heard that Rome was besieged. The City which had taken the whole world has itself been taken." This seemed to him to be the end of the world. Rome had endured for over a thousand years since its founding, but (he says) "Nothing is long which has an end." And he asks: "What is safe if Rome perishes?"

While we know nothing of the circumstances of the death of Pammachius, we have in one of Jerome's letters a detailed account of how Marcella met her fate.

In the interval of two years between her death and the writing of this eulogy, Jerome himself barely escaped death when an unexpected raid by Saracen bands who "like a torrent" overwhelmed Egypt, Palestine, Phoenicia, and Syria. If it is true, he remarks, that in wartime "the laws are silent," how much more does literature languish. For writing demands access to a library, and peace and quiet.

Quite appropriately, it seems to him, he is now at work on his commentary on the closing chapters of Ezechiel (Ezekiel), with the prophecies directed against Gog and Magog. The dire times, and his sadness of heart, are attuned to a consideration of the words of the gloomiest of the prophets. As he wrote he was frequently distracted by the need of caring for refugees. His old friend – and enemy – Rufinus is now dead; but heresy still lives.

In general this commentary is one of Jerome's best. He stresses the historical meaning of the prophet. There are interesting references to the present status of cities mentioned by the prophet. Tyre, whose mention brings to mind the illustrious names of Solomon's friend, King Hiram, of Dido, the founder of Carthage, and of Alexander the Great, was in Jerome's day the most beautiful and the richest city of Phoenicia. Syene (the modern Aswan) on the Egyptian frontier, was the farthest point that could be reached by ships, because the first cataract of the Nile is located there. Jerome states that there was an army post at Aswan in his time. The modern traveler is impressed by the size of an abandoned obelisk in the granite quarry there; because of a defect in the stone, it was never completed or removed.

Jerome was the first to realize that Tammuz, bewailed by the women in the Temple at Jerusalem, was the Adonis of the Phoenicians and the Greeks. "And he brought me in by the door of the gate of the Lord's house, which looked to the north," says Ezechiel (8:14), "and behold women sat there mourning for Adonis."

Here (as also in his commentary on Isaias) Jerome

stresses man's free will. God's foreknowledge, says Jerome, does not determine man's choice. But God knows in advance what man's free choice will be.

Such were the activities of body and of mind that distracted him in the two years that elapsed between the death of Marcella and the writing of his memorial to her in 412.

It was in her house on the Aventine Hill in Rome that Jerome had been accustomed to meet the circle of devout women who became his pupils in the study of Hebrew and of the Bible.

Jerome says to Principia that his two years' silence was due, not to any wish to hide his feelings, but his incredible grief has been so devastating that he judged it better to remain silent than to write anything unworthy of Marcella.

Left an orphan by her father's death, she was also widowed within a year of her marriage. Her mother Albina urged her to remarry, and favored a wealthy old man of high rank, who courted her. "If I had not determined to devote myself to perpetual chastity," said Marcella, "I would in any case seek a husband, not an inheritance"!

She lived a life free from scandal, dressed modestly, wore no jewelry, and was a devoted student of the Bible.

"At that time," says Jerome, "no lady of noble family in Rome knew of the monastic life." It was from some priests of Alexandria in Egypt and from Athanasius (who came to Rome when persecuted by the Arians) that she heard about Anthony, the first hermit. So Marcella and a number of her friends began to live at Rome in accordance with the monastic rule. Paula and Eustochium were inspired by her example. "It is easy," says Jerome, "to form an opinion about a teacher who had such pupils." All this took place before Jerome returned to Rome in 382.

When the needs of the Church had brought him to Rome — in response to a request made by Pope Damasus — Jerome says that he modestly avoided the gaze of ladies of high station. But Marcella's persistence overcame his timidity. He had some reputation (he tells us) as a student of Scripture, and whenever she met him Marcella had some question to ask about the Bible. She used to interpose objections so that she might learn from his answers what to say in reply to others.

Jerome says that she was an ideal student. She later became an authority on the meaning of Holy Writ, always, however, attributing what she said to the teachings of Jerome. She later gathered a group of women about her in the country outside of Rome. "I rejoiced," says Jerome, "that Rome had become a second Jerusalem."

After they were separated by Jerome's departure from Rome, they kept up their companionship by frequent letters.

When Origen's heretical doctrines were preached at Rome, Marcella was an outstanding supporter of the orthodox faith — though even Pope Siricius was deceived by false teaching. She challenged Macarius and Rufinus to defend their viewpoint; but apparently they refused to do so. "They preferred to be condemned in their absence rather than be shown to be guilty to their face," remarks Jerome. Then the storm of Origenism moved eastward to Jerusalem.

When Alaric took Rome in 410, "the blood-stained victors" burst into Marcella's house. They found Principia at her friend's side. After beating her to force her to reveal treasures she did not possess, "Christ softened their hard hearts." So the two ladies were escorted to the basilica of St. Paul. There she thanked God that the invaders had found her a poor woman — not made her one.

When she died peacefully a few months later, though sound in both mind and body, Marcella made Principia "the heir of her poverty" — bequeathing to her the care of the poor.

Jerome declares that he dictated this letter "in the wakeful hours of one short night" and that his sole desire was "to please God and my readers."

CHAPTER X - THE LAST DAYS

JEREMIAS was the last prophet remaining to be explained by a commentary. But Jerome did not live to complete this task; he died after writing six books, covering thirty-two of the fifty-two chapters. Like his commentary on Matthew, this work was dedicated to his friend Eusebius of Cremona. It will be remembered that it was he who had stayed in Bethlehem during the Origen controversy and supported Jerome against Rufinus.

We know of no commentary on Jeremias by Origen. He had, however, composed forty-five homilies, or discourses, on Jeremias. Jerome had translated fourteen of these into Latin while he was in Constantinople with Gregory of Nazianzus. In this commentary Jerome does not mention these homilies, probably because of his changed attitude to Rufinus — now almost universally branded as a heretic. He does make use of them, however. As he is now stressing historical interpretation and rejecting the allegorical, he cites Origen only to criticize him. He mentions no other sources, but says that he wishes to mediate to the Roman world the wisdom of the Hebrews.

At about this time religious controversy arose once more, now against a certain Pelagius, a native of Britain. Coming to Rome, he taught heretical doctrines. He denied both original sin (that is, guilt inherited from the disobedience of Adam) and the necessity of grace, God's favor, believing that man can fulfill God's commands by his own strength. After the sack of Rome in 410 by Alaric, Pelagius went to Carthage, where he was officially acquitted of the charge of heresy. But Augustine brought the matter before two synods, both of which condemned Pelagius' teaching. Rome concurred in these verdicts.

The entire commentary on the book of Jeremias is permeated by a polemic against Pelagianism. Jerome couples Pelagius with Rufinus, and declares that he is reviving the heresy of Origen, Jovinian, and Rufinus. All of them depend (he says) on the Pythagorean Sextus, whom Rufinus had translated into Latin and then deceitfully published under the name of the Roman pope and martyr Sixtus.

These times were filled with difficulties and hardships for Jerome. Many of his friends had died: Paula in 403; Pammachius and Marcella in 410; of his Roman friends, the only ones left were Oceanus, Principia, and Fabiola. Eustochium, who had succeeded her mother as head of the convent at Bethlehem, died in 418. She, in turn, was succeeded by the younger Paula.

Jerome's scholarship and wide knowledge are clearly revealed in a letter (106) he wrote possibly in or about 390. Two Gothic clergymen, Sunnia and Fretela, had written to ask Jerome how the discrepancies between the Gallican Psalter (which had become known to them) and the Greek text of the Psalter (which they were themselves using) were to be reconciled. Apparently the copy of the Latin translation which they had secured lacked the dia-

critical marks — the obelus and the asterisk — which Jerome
had introduced into his version. Because of a scribe's care-
lessness their copy was imperfect in this regard. Following
Origen's example, Jerome used the obelus ÷ to indicate
that a passage found in the Greek of the Septuagint was
not in the Hebrew text. In like manner, the asterisk * shows
the addition from the Hebrew of passages not included in
the Greek.

Jerome's oldest translation of the Psalms had been made
on very conservative principles, he tells these inquirers. By
citing specific passages, he indicates to them that elegance
and good taste when they do not run counter to the sense
are the true principles of translation. In the final chapter
of the letter (which is a long one), Jerome complies with
their request for Latin renderings of certain specific Greek
words whose meanings elude them. He also identifies for
them the Greek text which they have been using.

Jerome now defends a free rendering as contrasted with
a literal translation. In the New Testament, he says, we
turn to the Greek text in cases of doubt, but in the Old
Testament, when there are discrepancies between the Greek
and the Latin, we may reach the truth from the Hebrew.

This letter serves a double purpose, since it is also used
as a reply to Jerome's friend Avitus, who had frequently
asked him about the text of the Psalter. This Avitus may
be the same person who asked Jerome for a copy of his
translation of Origen's "First Principles." In reply, Jerome
sent him the literal translation — now lost — which he had
made at the request of Pammachius. He added also a list
of the heretical ideas in it. This letter to Avitus (Epistle

124) is important for the list of heresies which it contains.

The extant letters of this period in his life make it clear that Jerome was carrying on a heavy correspondence with people in Gaul, and was answering many questions dealing with the interpretation of scriptural passages. As a matter of fact, Jerome's commentary on the Apocalypse was an outgrowth of his correspondence with a man called Anatolius.

The disasters of the time — the sack of Rome and the breaking up of both government and home life, the destruction of property and the annihilation of whole families — turned men's minds everywhere to religion and to the peace of the religious life. Jerome repeatedly declares that the Christian must give up all that he has and follow Jesus. "Give it," he says, "not to your friends, not to your relatives, not to your kindred, not to your wife, not to your children — I shall add something more: do not reserve anything for yourself through fear of want." All must be given to the poor.

To a certain Julian, who had lost two young daughters within three weeks, and soon after his beloved wife Faustina as well, he advocates following the example of the holy Vera, who consecrated her life to God. Taking a text from Vergil, Jerome urges Julian to make this woman his guide, quoting the familiar words *dux femina facti.*

With similar intent, Jerome wrote to a widow named Ageruchia to dissuade her from a second marriage. Concluding with a vivid and stirring description of the downfall of the Roman Empire, he asks: How can Ageruchia think of marriage at such a time? Why her husband must either be a soldier or a deserter! He promises to dedicate to her a book on monogamy.

One of the most charming of all Jerome's letters is the old monk's kindly and understanding message to a little girl named Pacatula, who had been dedicated to God by her father before she was born. She must read this letter for herself in later years, he says, meanwhile studying the alphabet, spelling, grammar, and syntax! As she grows older, Pacatula is to commit to memory the Psalms, and treasure particularly the writings of Solomon, the Gospels, and the prophets.

In advocating a blameless life, Jerome cries: "For shame, the world is falling in ruins but our sins still flourish." Lamenting the times into which this child has been born, Jerome says: "She will know tears before laughter, she will feel sorrow before she knows joy." He declares that although she has scarcely appeared upon the stage, the curtain is about to fall.

This letter, like the opening chapters of Augustine's *Confessions*, shows a clear understanding of a child's outlook upon life.

Another letter written by Jerome in these later years may be compared with his famous epistle to Eustochium on celibacy. It is addressed to a young girl named Demetrias, who was contemplating renunciation of marriage in favor of the life of a nun. When she finally took the veil, after consulting both Augustine and Alypius in Africa, and with the full consent of her family, the noble line of the Anicii — extolled by the Gothic historian Jordanes — came to an end.

Although Jerome wrote many letters to his friends, and

translated Scripture as well, he never failed to take up arms against heresy. Thus, during his last years, we should not be surprised to find him attacking another heresy. This new enemy of the Church rejected the doctrine of original sin. Its official name is Pelagianism, named after its author, Pelagius.

PELAGIANISM

Pelagius, the Irish monk, had lived in Rome for a long time. When he went to Africa, in 411, his life took a tragic turn. He was now regarded as an arch heretic. His friend and pupil, Caelestius, had sought a priestly office in Africa, but was denounced in the year 411 by Deacon Paulinus of Milan.

Caelestius (who, like Pelagius, rejected the doctrine of original sin) based his doubts as to inherited guilt upon the writings of Rufinus.

Pelagius came to the Holy Land to visit Bishop John of Jerusalem. It will be recalled that John and Jerome had been bitterly opposed on the question of Origenism. In spite of their reconciliation, relations between the two were strained at best. Now, while he was visiting in Palestine, Pelagius criticized Jerome's commentary on Ephesians. Thereupon Jerome called him a pupil of Rufinus, made fun of his Scotch-Irish ancestry, and declared that oatmeal had dulled his wits!

When Jerome was informed of the state of affairs in Africa by two letters from Augustine, delivered to him by Orosius, he broke off his earlier friendship with Pelagius. Although these two long letters mention neither Pelagius nor Caelestius, Augustine raises two questions in them: (1) as to the origin of the soul; and (2) on the identity of all sins.

Ever since the Origen controversy, the question as to the origin of the soul had been in the forefront of theological controversy. Three solutions of the problem had been suggested:

1. Creationism — that individual souls are newly created by God for each created person.

2. Traducianism — the doctrine of inherited guilt.

3. The theory of pre-existence.

The third of these had been declared heretical. The Pelagians, rejecting inherited guilt, believed in Creationism. Caelestius was the first to write against Traducianism.

An imperial commissioner named Marcellinus had been conducting discourses on religion with the Donatists in Carthage. The civil power had been called in by the Church to crush this new schism. Marcellinus decided in favor of the Catholic position. He then turned to Jerome for the solution of a difficult question, namely: "How can Creationism — the theory which he personally accepted — be reconciled with the assumption of inherited guilt?"

In a reply addressed to Marcellinus and Anapsychias (who is otherwise unknown), Jerome refers to his writings against Rufinus. He recommends also that they consult Oceanus on the question or — if they want an answer by word of mouth — Augustine, who is near at hand.

They took this last advice. But Augustine was himself uncertain, and turned to Jerome for help! "You have sent me pupils," he says, "whom I am to teach a matter which

I have not yet learned! Teach me, therefore, what I am to teach." The question has been raised by others, and his friends are beginning to say to him: "Are you a teacher of Israel, and yet you do not understand this?" Augustine says that it gives him more pleasure to hear a teacher — in this case, Jerome — than to be heard as a teacher himself.

Augustine goes on to state his firm conviction that the human soul is immortal and incorporeal. It has sinned — through no fault of God, but of its own free will. The soul will be freed from sin by the grace of God, in Jesus Christ.

Now Augustine asks Jerome to tell him whence the soul has received this inherited guilt which leads to damnation. He is convinced that such inherited guilt does have sway over all mankind — including infants who die unbaptized.

If we accept the belief called Creationism — that individual souls are newly created by God — why should newborn babes that die unbaptized be damned, having committed no sin? For God condemns no sinless soul. This is the gist of the first of the two letters which Jerome received from his great contemporary.

In the second, written at the same time, Augustine asks Jerome's opinion of the statement made by James (2:10): "whoever keeps the whole law, but offends in one point, has become guilty in all." Apparently Pelagius and his followers relied on this text. Augustine wishes to know how this compares with the Stoic doctrine of the identity of all sins, for Pelagius based his point of view on ancient ethics, and in particular upon the Stoic doctrine.

In the closing paragraph of this letter Augustine pays Jerome the compliment of high praise, which is, of course, all the more significant because it comes from so great a theologian. Augustine declares that, in the Lord's name, and by His aid, ecclesiastical literature has profited more through Jerome than through any previous writer. Evidently their earlier misunderstanding has now been completely cleared up.

Before he answered this letter, Jerome (in the spring of 415) had entered the Pelagian controversy by his letter to Ctesiphon. He was a Roman, whose family was on intimate and cordial terms with Pelagius. Jerome took advantage of a question raised by Ctesiphon to speak out openly against this new heresy without mentioning either Pelagius or Caelestius.

The statement of Pelagius assailed by Jerome was that man can attain sinless perfection. Thus, Jerome asks, "For if once man can be without sin by his own effort, what need is there of God's grace?" On the other hand, if man needs God's grace, why say he can do what he manifestly cannot?

Jerome's own position is not that of Augustine. Jerome believes that free will depends upon God's grace: "for God is at work in you, both to will and to work for his good pleasure." Jerome challenges Pelagius to cite examples of righteous persons who have not sinned.

In his attack Jerome sought to point out that Pelagianism was merely a continuation of the heretical doctrines of Origen and of Jovinian — which had already been condemned.

In a synod held at Jerusalem in 415, Pelagius was accused of the Origenist heresy. His friend John of Jerusalem pre-

sided over the meeting. Pelagius, who spoke Greek, defended himself with great skill. He declared that he agreed
completely with the Greek fathers. As for his pupil Caelestius, he disclaimed all responsibility for what he said.

Orosius was sent to Palestine by Augustine, but as he
was familiar only with Latin he found himself unable to
cope with the situation. Pelagius was acquitted.

In December of the same year (415) an accusation by
two deposed Western bishops who were now in Palestine
led to a new hearing, to be held at Diospolis — known also
as Lydda — in Palestine. In anticipation of this meeting
Jerome wrote his fine dialogue directed against the Pelagians. It was a detailed rebuttal of their position. Augustine
praised this as a work of wondrous beauty, and said it was
on a higher level than his previous controversial writings directed against Origen, Helvidius, Jovinian, and Vigilantius.

Influenced by Augustine, Jerome now assumes an inherited guilt which must be atoned by Baptism. This marks
a change in his views. Baptism is necessary (Jerome now
says) because their parents' sins are visited upon them —
even though they themselves have not sinned. We are reminded of the question asked of Jesus by his disciples:
"Rabbi, who has sinned, this man or his parents, that he
should be born blind?"

In the third book of this dialogue the question of pre-
destination and the necessity of infant baptism is taken
up. No human being is completely without sin, says Jerome.
God alone is sinless.

However, when the synod met to deal with the case of
Pelagius, its members — dissenting from Jerome's view —

agreed with Pelagius that with God's aid a man may be sinless. Pelagius then expressly stated his belief in the Trinity and was acquitted of heresy. Jerome laments that Pelagius has denied all the things that he was known to have done.

In 416, Orosius returned to Augustine, carrying a letter from Jerome in which he excused himself for inability to answer the two questions at the time, because of his absorption in the Pelagian controversy. He explains that he did not want to express any difference of opinion which might lead detractors to say that he and Augustine were not in accord.

THE AFTERMATH AND JEROME'S DEATH

Not long after Orosius' departure with the letter to Augustine, the followers of Pelagius visited their wrath upon Jerome. A horde of fanatical monks attacked the monastery in Bethlehem, killing monks and nuns, murdering a deacon, and setting fire to the building. Our knowledge of this outrage comes from a writing of Augustine on the deeds of Pelagius.

In all likelihood Pelagius himself was not the instigator of this attack, however, though Bishop John of Jerusalem seems to have been implicated. So Jerome wrote to Bishop Aurelius of Carthage, who was a friend of Augustine, in order to bring the matter to the attention of Pope Innocent and to have proceedings started against Bishop John.

Jerome wrote to Riparius immediately after the Pelagian assault on Bethlehem (which occurred toward the close of the year 416), saying that it has seemed best to him to leave the place (Bethlehem) rather than suffer the true faith to be contaminated by association with heretics.

Pope Innocent sent Jerome a letter of consolation by Bishop Aurelius. He said, however, that since the perpetrators were unknown, nothing could be done. He added that Bishop John had assured him that nothing of the kind would occur again in the churches over which he exercised control.

Pope Innocent wrote Bishop John a letter of censure, saying that Eustochium and Paula have accused the devil of employing robbery, murder, and arson in their church. They mentioned no man as being the instigator of these crimes. The pope adds that although there can be no doubt as to the guilty person, the protection which John should have furnished appears to have been lacking. "I have heard," he adds, "that the Lord's flock and such lambs [as Eustochium and Paula] exposed to fire, armed attack and persecution, and without defense, are barely dragging out their existence after the murder and death of members of their household." He points out that the devil has scored a victory against the bishop himself in bringing these disasters upon a church under his jurisdiction. John died early in 417 — perhaps before he received this letter from the pope.

Jerome learned that both Pelagius and his pupil Caelestius had been condemned at an African synod held in 416. Thereupon he wrote to congratulate Augustine, saying that orthodox Catholics venerate him as a second founder of the faith, and — an even greater distinction — all the heretics detest him!

Pelagius left Jerusalem and disappeared. There is a figurative reference to his death — or perhaps to the death of Bishop John: Jerome says that the heretic, unwilling to listen to Jeremiah, prefers to go to Egypt to die at Daphne.

Writing to Apronius, Jerome reports that all is now calm once more. And though he grieves over the destruction of all his earthly possessions, he still has spiritual riches. "It is better to eat bread," he says, "than to lose one's faith."

Jerome's old friend, Eusebius of Cremona, brought him a reply (no longer extant) to his dialogue by Deacon Annianus of Celeda. In writing to Augustine and Alypius about it, he refers to the author as "the pseudo-deacon," and declares his intention of writing an answer. He did not live to do this.

Before his death he had the further sorrow of losing his dear friend Eustochium.

Prosper's Chronicle states that Jerome died on September 30, 420.

These are the chief events in the life of Jerome, as seen through his own eyes and either related or referred to in his letters. Unfortunately he was not, it seems, a lover of nature, and has little to say of the places where he lived. He was impressed, however, by the desert and by the sea. His references to contemporary events are chiefly incidental, and occur particularly in the introductions to his commentaries on the books of the Bible. After translating the *Chronicle* of Eusebius of Caesarea from Greek into Latin, he added enough to bring the record down to his own time — much as Confucius did in his "Spring and Autumn."

The first of his extant letters (dealing with the woman

who miraculously escaped death, though struck seven times by the executioner's sword) was written in 370 at Aquileia.

Letters two, three, and four were written at Antioch before he entered the desert as a hermit. The interesting epistles from the desert of Chalcis (5–17 inclusive) cover the years from 374 to 379.

While in Constantinople, from May to July of 381, Jerome wrote, for Pope Damasus, his detailed exegesis of Isaias, chapter 6. This has come down to us in the form of a letter (18), although it is not an actual letter but an interpretation of a passage of Scripture, lacking both the normal introductory remarks and the conclusion that one would expect in a letter. It covers about thirty printed pages, and is subdivided into two parts called XVIII A and XVIII B in Hilberg's edition.

Letters 19–25 inclusive were written from Rome during the three years of Jerome's stay there (382–385).

The remainder of his published correspondence, letters 46–148, covers the period of his stay in Bethlehem (386–419). He died, as has been said, in 420.

We become aware as we read his letters that in spite of an essentially kind and loving nature Jerome was subject to outbursts of anger. There are many abusive passages and sarcastic utterances in his writings. As regards criticism of himself, Jerome once said: "If you want to correct me when I'm at fault, reprove me openly. Only don't criticize me behind my back. For how will it help me if you tell other people my faults?" It is rather touching to see how he is willing to assume that the motive of such criticism is a desire to help.

We look in vain for real humor in Jerome's writings, although there are occasional playful passages. We are impressed by his interest in people and his willingness to be of service to others.

Friends meant much to Jerome, and many of his letters are actually eulogies of the departed — brief biographies in epistolary form. Such are his letters dealing with Blesilla, Nepotian; Fabiola; with Marcella; and Paula. In these letters in particular are to be found philosophical passages, like that in his letter to Heliodorus on the untimely death of the young priest Nepotian. This was written in 396, after the sack of Rome; Jerome sought to console his old friend by pointing to the general misery of the times. "We are not alone," he says, in effect. He calls attention to a world in ruins, the barbarian tribes on the move, the downfall of kingdoms. So in antiquity had his friend Servilius tried to comfort Cicero for the loss of his daughter by referring to the flourishing cities of antiquity which were now only masses of rubble.

Were we to ascend into a watchtower high enough to afford a bird's-eye view of the whole world (says Jerome), we would see some men being tortured, some enslaved, some drowned at sea. He reminds his friend that man is mortal and all earth's present inhabitants are soon to pass away. "Words fail me," he says. "This theme is too great. All I have said is inadequate."

After all, it was this contrast between the temporal and the eternal, between the earthly Babylon and the heavenly Jerusalem that had induced Jerome to forsake the world and live in the hope of the joys of paradise. Those who have fallen asleep in the Lord are only that much farther advanced than their friends who still toil in this vale of tears. As St. Paul puts it: "For to me to live is Christ and to die is gain." Jerome was convinced of the truth of this statement and sought to apply it to his own life.